THE WINTER'S TALE:
A STUDY

By the same author

SHAKESPEARE AND THE POPULAR
DRAMATIC TRADITION

THE WINTER'S TALE:

A STUDY

By S. L. BETHELL

M.A. (CANTAB.)

*Lecturer in English
in the University College of South Wales
and Monmouthshire*

NEW YORK   TORONTO

STAPLES PRESS LIMITED

CAVENDISH PLACE, LONDON, W1

BOOK
PRODUCTION
WAR ECONOMY
STANDARD

*This book is produced in complete
conformity with the authorised
economy standards*

SET IN MONOTYPE BASKERVILLE SERIES

Made and printed in England by
STAPLES PRESS LIMITED
at their St. Albans, Herts, establishment

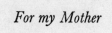

For my Mother

CONTENTS

N.B.—*The Globe edition has been used for all Shakespearean references and quotations.*

INTRODUCTION

IN MY BOOK *Shakespeare and the Popular Dramatic Tradition*[1]
I tried to show that the plays of Shakespeare are com-
pounded in varying proportions of the elements of con-
ventionalism and naturalism and that the Elizabethan
audience must have reacted to them in a much more
complex way than is required of the audience at a modern
'serious' play written on the principles of photographic
realism. The popular audience in a contemporary cinema
or music-hall, unconcerned with theories of dramatic art,
finds no difficulty in accepting the most 'impossible' conventions: unseen orchestras strike up and characters
break suddenly into song; pure farce may mingle with
domestic tragedy; a stage show occurring in a film may
develop into a performance that no real theatre could
possibly contain. If this is true of the popular audience
after a century in which the tendency to naturalism or
realism has been persistent, in philosophy, in painting,
in the novel and in the drama itself (for the reactions of
impressionism, expressionism and so forth have been
limited to 'highbrow' circles), we may well expect that in
Elizabethan times the ready acceptance of conventions
and the complexity of response which that acceptance
entails would be natural to all who attended the theatre.
Even apart from the drama, the Elizabethans seem to have
enjoyed the exercise of keeping diverse aspects of a situation in mind at the same time; hence their love of the
'conceit', in which heterogeneous objects are brought into
an intellectual union, and of allegory, in which an outer
and an inner meaning must be simultaneously perceived.
The Christian tradition with its reconciliation of opposites
– God and man in Our Lord, spirit and matter in the
sacraments – provides the immediate source of this type

[1] King and Staples, 1944.

of thinking, but it goes behind the Christian revelation
and is rooted in the complex nature of man himself. In
late Elizabethan and Jacobean times, however, it grew
momentarily more explicit, partly to comprehend the cultural tension between the Christian tradition and revived
classicism and partly in conscious or unconscious opposition to the spiritualist and materialist monisms which were
issuing from the renewed interest in Greek thought.

On one side of its development the Elizabethan drama
emerges directly out of the miracle plays and moralities,
in which conventions were obvious and abundant: characters announced their own names and functions in the
plot; the stage could be divided (in the miracles) to represent different localities; the stage personages (in the
moralities) might personify abstractions such as Truth,
Good Deeds, Gluttony, Lechery. Yet these conventional
plays contained passages of the most direct realism, as,
for example, the professional indifference and crude
jesting of the soldiers at the erection of the Cross.[1] Alto-
gether, they seem to have demanded of their simple
audience a moderately complex mode of attention. The
Elizabethan drama added to this complexity by uniting
the medieval tradition with the classical, so that new
conventions and new types of realism fused with the old,
yet without quite annihilating their qualitative differences;
the Elizabethan audience had to think in the Plautus-
Seneca and the miracle-morality contexts at the same time.
They could do this, not because they were particularly
learned or imaginative or intense but because the dramatic
development had proceeded naturally in the atmosphere
of the theatre and their responses were uncontaminated
by theory and so operated below the level of self-conscious
thought. It is only as abstract thinkers that most of us are
simple-minded; in the areas of the mind where activity is

[1] *V.* The Pynneres (and Paynters) *Crucifixio Cristi* in the York Plays, ed. Lucy
Toulmin Smith (Clarendon Press, 1885), pp. 349 *et seq.*; also The Crucifixion
in the Towneley Plays, ed. George England (Early English Text Society,
1897), pp. 258 *et seq.*

spontaneous we can perform remarkable feats of apprehension without being aware that anything in particular
is going on. So the Elizabethans were able to attend to a
number of different aspects of a situation simultaneously
yet without confusion: they were aware of the balcony as
Juliet's balcony and as a part of the auditorium; they
recognised Burbage as Burbage and accepted him as the
Prince of Denmark; they took the First Player's speech as
serious for Hamlet, though intended for them as a burlesque of the old-fashioned drama. This was the common
playhouse situation for an Elizabethan dramatist, meaning
very little to most of them, no doubt, but producing in
the hands of surpassing genius a poetic drama which in its
depth and breadth of perception, its complex unity of
vision, defeats all ultimate analysis and ranges the critic
with the common file in humility and wonder.

How far Shakespeare himself knew what he was doing
when he exploited so remarkably the apparent ineptitudes
of his 'wooden O' is a question we can never decide. But,
whether he knew it or not, it was the 'multi-consciousness'
of the Elizabethan audience – an inelegant term, perhaps,
but I can find no better – which provided him with the
opportunity to express his subtle and profound reading of
experience, his ordered vision of multiplicity in unity.
And so in approaching a play of Shakespeare we have to
bear simultaneously in mind the duality of real world and
play world; the duality of time in the contrast of historic
setting and contemporary reference; the duality of overt
action and implied meaning; and the ambiguity of comedy
and tragedy, for both these aspects of reality can be found
together in a sort of counterpoint, as in the graveyard
scene in *Hamlet* or the tragic humour of Lear's mock trial
of his daughters: 'I here take my oath before this honourable assembly, she kicked the poor king her father'
(III. vi. 48).

In *Shakespeare and the Popular Dramatic Tradition* my aim
was to present a critical approach to Shakespeare based

upon these considerations, and my treatment of the plays
was only illustrative and incidental. My present aim is to
concentrate upon one play and to see how far 'the principle
of multi-consciousness' will take us towards an understanding of its complexity. I have chosen *The Winter's
Tale* because it seems to me to be a very important and
highly successful play, because it is unusually complex
even for Shakespeare and because it has been curiously
neglected by the generality of critics. Perhaps I should say
something here about the element of Christian dogma in
my interpretation of this and other plays of Shakespeare,
since this aspect of my former book met with adverse
criticism in certain quarters. I should have thought that
the relevant question was that of Shakespeare's religion,
not mine. It seems, however, to have been assumed that
I gave a Christian interpretation of *King Lear* and *Antony
and Cleopatra* because I happen to be a churchman myself.
Is this intended to imply that a 'humanist' interpretation
of Shakespeare would be equally the result of intellectual
bias – that it is impossible to attain anything like an
objective view of Shakespeare's position? Or is it only the
churchman whose judgment is warped by his beliefs?
For my own part I should say that it is next to impossible
for any one now to interpret a Shakespeare play with
precisely the balance of interests with which an Elizabethan
would have approached it. But is there any need for us to
obtain an Elizabethan point of view? Perhaps we are in a
position to get more out of Shakespeare to-day than his
contemporaries were. I do not mean that the play itself is
neutral and that we read into it what we will. Quite the
contrary. But poetry – especially Shakespeare's poetry –
has so many inwoven meanings; there is more implied in
a passage of Shakespeare than any contemporary could
consciously understand, more surely than Shakespeare
himself deliberately intended, and certainly more than
any one modern reader can properly discern. Our task,
necessarily a co-operative one, is to draw out as much of

Shakespeare's meaning as we can, and each of us will tend to be impressed by an aspect related to his own interests. If we have had Shakespeare the botanist and Shakespeare the horse-leech, why not Shakespeare the theologian? If he has any theology at all, it is likely in its very nature to be more regulative of his thought than many other fields of knowledge in which the critics have joyously disported themselves. I find it difficult to understand why certain writers are convinced that Shakespeare cannot have seriously held the dogmas of Christianity. Is it because their own humanistic way of thinking has become so natural to them that they mistake *its* dogmas for the laws of nature and think that all well-disposed persons must be of their party? The Christian in modern times is sufficiently aware of his beliefs as differing from established tradition; he is the less likely to take things for granted and to assume that others, including Shakespeare, must necessarily be Christian also. The critic who is self-consciously aware of holding a particular view of life is much less prone to fall into error than he who believes himself 'impartial', 'scientific', a 'pure scholar', for the latter as a human being must have some sort of embryonic philosophy concealed somewhere about him – and presumably it lurks in his 'subconscious', beyond his volitional control, pulling and tugging at the judgment which he believes quite free from such invalid interference.

My own view is that Shakespeare was a Christian, either a Roman Catholic recusant, as Smart believed his father to have been,[1] or an Anglican inclining more to Hooker than to Calvin. An accumulation of evidence in comparatively recent publications[2] makes the latter hypothesis seem much the more likely. I do not think, however, that

[1] *V.* John Semple Smart: *Shakespeare: Truth and Tradition* (Arnold, 1928), pp. 66-72.
[2] *V.* Alfred Hart: *Shakespeare and the Homilies* (Melbourne University Press, 1934); Richmond Noble: *Shakespeare's Biblical Knowledge, and Use of the Book of Common Prayer* (S.P.C.K., 1935); T. W. Baldwin: *William Shakspere's Petty School* (University of Illinois Press, 1943).

any theory as to Shakespeare's theological beliefs can rise
above the status of probable opinion; the plays are plays,
not propaganda, and they have the 'impersonality' of great
art, the impersonality which comes not, indeed, of crushing
but of expanding and universalising the personality of the
author. I should say, then, that the interpretation of life
that Shakespeare presents is a profoundly Christian interpretation, one, that is, which harmonises exactly with the
Christian scheme, and I should also assert that a number of
Christian ideas and theological terms are used by Shakespeare with accuracy and insight. But I should not be
prepared to say that this necessarily implies that Shakespeare was himself a practising churchman. The culture
of Elizabethan and Jacobean England was a Christian
culture; Shakespeare belongs to it and is in no sense in
rebellion against it. His plays are a poetic crystallisation
of that culture at its greatest height and depth; if he is
also the most profoundly human writer in our literature,
that may be an argument for the validity of the culture
which he reflects. Perhaps his poetic vision was never
completely formulated in theological terms. It is even
theoretically possible that he was not a professing Christian,
though this would require a divorce between private
opinion and public expression almost unthinkable in a
poet and would involve the remarkable, yet not impossible,
corollary that his unconscious attitudes are those of his
publicly expressed and not of his privately entertained
beliefs. In any event, my concern is with expressed beliefs
and unconscious attitudes, and all my reading of the plays
has gone to confirm my opinion that Shakespeare wrote
consistently from the standpoint of orthodox Christianity.

PART ONE

Place, Time and Reality

I – PRELIMINARY

RELATIVELY LITTLE has been written about Shakespeare's late romances. This last period of his dramatic activity has been labelled 'Autumn' and the critics seem to have found it as much a season of mists as of the mellow fruitfulness which they have feelingly extolled. The half-symbolic heroines were admired by the Victorians for their ingenuous young girlhood, but a later generation preferred the decent veil of sophisticated wit in which Beatrice, Rosalind and Viola draped their maiden modesty. Reactions against the more general sentiment of 'Autumn' or 'On the Heights' are to be found in Lytton Strachey's view of late Shakespeare as a bored and disillusioned artist, to whom nothing matters but a rhythm or a turn of phrase, and the historical school's sharp business-man who 'cashed in' on a new popular demand created by Beaumont and Fletcher. But great poetry cannot be spun spider-fashion out of its own bowels and there is no ivory-towered seclusion about the verse of these plays. As for the historical school, they account perhaps correctly for a superficial resemblance to the Beaumont and Fletcher romances but make no attempt to account for a deeper dissimilarity which they may not have noticed.

Though they are still somewhat sparingly dealt with, there have been signs in recent years of an awakening interest in the group of plays from *Pericles* to *The Tempest*. Dr. E. M. W. Tillyard, in *Shakespeare's Last Plays*,[1] has produced a brief but important study which I have found most helpful, especially in its discussion of 'planes of reality'. Unfortunately, *The Winter's Tale* does not receive close treatment, although justice is done to its merits and

[1] Chatto and Windus, 1938.

significance; Dr. Tillyard has abandoned the old view of
the play as merely the last stepping-stone to the triumph of
The Tempest. Since the eighteenth century *The Winter's
Tale* has been fairly popular on the stage, though usually
in condensed and garbled versions, but no Shakespearean
scholar has made it the subject of a book, and even short
essays are infrequent. In 1937 an extremely interesting
and valuable article on the play was contributed by the
late F. C. Tinkler to the periodical *Scrutiny*[1]; I have made
much use of it in the following pages. In general, Tinkler
brings out the contrasting themes of sophistication and
rural simplicity which he sees exemplified in the court
of Leontes and the pastoral life of Bohemia; these different
modes of living have to be amalgamated in order to attain
a stable and satisfactory culture. The story of Leontes is
seen almost as a version of the Waste Land legend, the
sterile king being restored to his former way of life by the
return of his daughter, Perdita, who stands as a symbol of
life-giving nature. King and country are essentially one, and
the 'heirless kingdom' regains its health by the same means.
The renewed friendship of Bohemia and Sicilia represents
the successful fusion of court sophistication and country
simplicity, so that social theory dovetails into the theme of
'dying into life'. It is impossible here to do justice to the
careful examination of the text from which these generalisa-
tions are derived. Tinkler seems to be aware of a certain
religious significance in the play, but his interpretation is
in terms not of Christian dogma but of an inherited
paganism related to the vegetation myths which have
grown popular since Mr. Eliot drew attention to Miss
Weston's book *From Ritual to Romance* in his notes on *The
Waste Land*. I am far from denying this 'pagan' strain in
The Winter's Tale, but pagan tradition was subsumed
under Christianity and transformed by it a great many
centuries before Shakespeare, and to my mind *The Winter's*

---

[1] Vol. V, No. 4 (March, 1937), pp. 344-364. The author's regrettably early
death was referred to in the same journal, Vol. X, No. 4 (April, 1942).

Tale presents only a further development of the process of transformation which produced the Church's year; the dominant note is that of supernatural religion. The case for a pagan tradition is rendered more plausible in Tinkler's article by two errors in interpretation which are so trivial in themselves that it seems ungrateful to mention them. I must do so, however, since they are bound up with the vital question of Shakespeare's religious attitudes in these last plays. The old Shepherd, dismayed at the love between Florizel and Perdita, feels that he may no longer die in peace in his own ancestral bed:

> . . . but now
> Some hangman must put on my shroud and lay me
> Where no priest shovels in dust.   (IV. iv. 467)

Tinkler comments: 'No explicitly religious sanctions are invoked (the priest is hardly more than a sexton) but, rather, if a label must be given to it, this attitude is that "Buddhist union of God and Death" which Mr. Empson finds in the novels of T. F. Powys'.[1] A note in the *Arden Shakespeare*[2] refers us at this point to the first Prayer Book of Edward VI (1549). I have confirmed the reference, which in the original reads: '*Then the priest castyng earth upon the Corps, shall saye.* I commende thy soule',[3] etc. The old Shepherd was a little behind the times in not having accustomed himself to the changed rubric of the Elizabethan Prayer Book – and perhaps country parsons were recalcitrant in such matters of traditional ceremony – but there is no suggestion that his religion savoured of vegetation cults or of Mr. Empson on Mr. Powys. I do not think that the next point was intended to support the pagan theory but it might have that effect. Tinkler says that to Hermione 'violent death is but a bug used by a

---

[1] *Loc. cit.*, p. 351.
[2] *The Winter's Tale*, ed. F. W. Moorman (Methuen, 1912), p. 89.
[3] So the reprint *verbatim et literatim* in *The Ancient and Modern Library of Theological Literature*. There are insignificant differences in the version given in the *Arden Shakespeare*.

nasty little boy to frighten little girls'.[1] Again the *Arden*
edition has a useful comment; so has Johnson's Dictionary where, after 'bug' defined as 'A stinking insect bred
in old household stuff', we move on to 'bug' coupled with
'bugbear': 'A frightful object; a walking spectre, imagined
to be seen; generally now used for a false terrour to frighten
babes'. It is in this latter connection that Johnson quotes
Hermione: 'The bug which you would fright me with I
seek' (III. ii. 93). Certainly death to Hermione is 'a false
terrour to frighten babes', but it is envisaged not as a
stinking insect but as a supernatural visitant. Her attitude
is one not of Stoic or Epicurean contempt but of Christian
resignation, a distinction of fundamental importance for a
proper understanding of the play.

II – THE MAIN PROBLEM
AND THE SIGNIFICANCE OF THE VERSE

WHY DOES Shakespeare in the last phase of his dramatic
activity turn to these naïve and impossible romances?
And why is his dramatic technique apparently crude and
incoherent? Was his interest waning – in the drama, or
in life? Was his technical ability deserting him? These
are the questions which every critic of the last plays
must attempt to answer and on which I hope my consideration of *The Winter's Tale* may cast some light; for,
though I propose to limit myself to the one play, my
argument applies in part to everything from *Pericles* to
The Tempest.

The quality of the verse shows that Shakespeare has not
lost interest in life. If the romances are far from the workaday world in their general outline, the workaday world
is nevertheless present everywhere through imagery and
reference. The verse is remarkably free, with rhythms
derived from impassioned speech superimposed upon the

[1] *Loc. cit.*, p. 360.

regular metric pattern, though there is sufficient regularity
to keep the pattern in the reader's or hearer's mind. The
rhythms are derived from impassioned speech but they are
not direct speech rhythms such as we find at times in
King Lear:

> Pray, do not mock me:
> I am a very foolish fond old man,
> Fourscore and upward, not an hour more nor less;
> And, to deal plainly,
> I fear I am not in my perfect mind.   (IV. vii. 59)

In *The Winter's Tale* the rhythms are twisted and contorted, neither smooth verse nor normal speech but a
rhythmic equivalent of complex thought or distorting
passion, though smoothed out occasionally by the religious
motive, in the repentance of Leontes and in his reunion
with Hermione. There is an unusual compression of
meaning, conveyed in broken syntax and elliptical expression, and a use of imagery and conceit more Jacobean than
Elizabethan. Shakespeare has been moving with the times
and his imagery is often purely functional, without intrinsic
beauty and wholly an instrument of impassioned thought,
though the Elizabethan freshness remains along with the
Donne-like conceit, and Perdita's flower speech has a
richness and purity which recalls yet transcends the 'nature
poetry' of *A Midsummer Night's Dream.* The language
throughout the play is especially concrete even for
Shakespeare:

> If therefore you dare trust my honesty,
> That lies enclosed in this trunk which you
> Shall bear along impawn'd, away to-night!
>   (I. ii. 434)

Honesty itself is given a location within the body. Mr.
Granville-Barker speaks of a 'new Euphuism' in these last
plays[1]; unlike the Euphuism of *Love's Labour's Lost*, however, it is no mere surface decoration but essential to the

---

[1] *Prefaces to Shakespeare, Second Series* (Sidgwick and Jackson, 1930), p. 288.

full statement of the author's experience. In the earlier play the young Shakespeare enjoyed the exercise of wit for its own sake; in *The Winter's Tale* he is no longer interested in his own cleverness but is entirely concerned with the depths of meaning revealed in his mature experience of life. The Petrarchan conceit (e.g., glances as arrows from Cupid's bow, the eyebrow) has a certain fanciful propriety yet always remains *appliqué*, whereas many of the conceits in late Shakespeare and Donne serve to bring together heterogeneous objects and modes of experience in a unifying process of thought:

> . . . and therefore, like a cipher,
> Yet standing in rich place, I multiply
> With one 'We thank you' many thousands moe
> That go before it.   (II. ii. 6)

A whole wide, varied world is revealed through the imagery alone: from crab-apples (I. ii. 102) to hat-blocks (I. ii. 225), from the lamb (I. ii. 67) to the spider (II. i. 40), from 'Sir Smile', the cuckold-maker (I. ii. 196) to the 'penitent reform'd' (I. ii. 239):

> No; if I mistake
> In those foundations which I build upon,
> The centre is not big enough to bear
> A school-boy's top—   (II. i. 100)

this bringing together of the earth's centre and a school-boy's top is quite typical. Moreover, such references are strictly contemporary, as are the colloquial forms:

> They're here with me already, whispering, rounding
> 'Sicilia is a so-forth': 'tis far gone,
> When I shall gust it last.   (I. ii. 217)

As in the later tragedies, there is little attempt to indicate character by giving a particular type of verse permanently to a particular stage personage. The old Shepherd certainly has a broad, slow rhythm and an appropriate

simplicity of language, but this is exceptional. There is less
difference in the quality of the verse between Leontes and
Perdita than between Leontes jealous and Leontes
penitent. Apart from the old Shepherd, all share the
rhythmic complexity, the wide range of imagery, the
ambiguity and ellipsis; these are characteristic of Shakespeare, not Leontes. To have differentiated character by
means of the verse would have meant sacrificing complexity whenever a simple-natured character holds the
stage and, as (to anticipate) the characters in these late
romances are less important as persons than as symbols
and what they are is much less important than what they
say, Shakespeare normally conveys character only through
meaning and not in external form – except for the old
Shepherd whose rural common sense and simple piety
are at times thrown into relief by a type of verse relatively
nearer to ordinary speech. There is no need to ascribe any
intellectual subtlety to Florizel, yet his love-making has
even more intellectual complexity than the jealousy of
Leontes. A mere description of his mistress' hand produces
a surprising collocation of images:

> I take thy hand, this hand,
> As soft as dove's down and as white as it,
> Or Ethiopian's tooth, or the fann'd snow that's bolted
> By the northern blasts twice o'er.   (IV. iv. 373)

'Bolted' introduces a metaphor into the simile and supplies
the further image of 'wheaten flour'; the snow is made
purer by being twice sifted as wheaten flour is sifted of its
impurities.

We may take another love-speech earlier in the same
scene:

> What you do
> Still betters what is done. When you speak, sweet,
> I'ld have you do it ever: when you sing,
> I'ld have you buy and sell so, so give alms,
> Pray so; and, for the ordering your affairs,

> To sing them too: when you do dance, I wish you
> A wave o' the sea, that you might ever do
> Nothing but that; move still, still so,
> And own no other function: each your doing,
> So singular in each particular,
> Crowns what you are doing in the present deeds,[1]
> That all your acts are queens.   (IV. iv. 135)

Except for an unusually complex ambiguity this passage
is fairly representative of the verse used in *The Winter's
Tale*; it is pleasantly evocative where Leontes is often
unpleasantly so but in method it is not unlike the Leontes
speeches. The free and varied rhythm suggests a pressure
of thought greater than the occasion would seem to require.
The whole speech is a single conceit, summed up in the
last three and a half lines. The first six lines introduce the
serious world of buying and selling, praying and giving
alms into a lover's fancy and so strengthen it into more
than fancy; an ideal attitude which is capable of application to the real. The association of Perdita's dance with the
sea is rhythmically enforced by a line shortened by a foot
to allow of long, sustained syllables: 'move still, still so' –
a wave motion, up and down, with the two 'stills' upon the
crest.[2] The unconscious effect of this, one of nature's
simplest and most fundamental rhythms, is to associate not
only Perdita's dancing but the whole spring festival with
the sea, so that Perdita in her dual relationship to the sea
and the spring season grows poetically into a symbol of
life and creative energy – a compound of Flora, as Florizel
has already named her, with an Aphrodite chastened by
prayer and almsgiving. The sea is also a traditional image
of the mind with its emotional calm and storm; a storm at
sea is of central importance in *The Winter's Tale* as well as
in *Pericles* and *The Tempest*.

---

[1] I have restored 'deeds', the reading of all early editions. Spedding's 'deed',
which stands in the *Globe* edition, is without authority and seeks to simplify
the Shakespearean ambiguity.

[2] This has been noted by the Cowden-Clarkes; *v. The Variorum Shakespeare*,
ed. Horace Howard Furness (Philadelphia, 1898), Vol. XI, p. 201.

|The last three and a half lines restate more carefully
what is said in the first two, and the whole statement has
an interesting ambiguity. The first two lines may be taken
as meaning: 'Whatever you do is done the better because
it is you who do it' (i.e., 'you bring a new grace to every
action'); or we may render it: 'Each of your acts is better
than the preceding'; or again, straining the meaning a
little: 'Your performance of any action is better than that
of others'. Correspondingly, the last three and a half
lines may mean: 'Now, in your present actions (i.e., 'in
the present deeds'), everything you do, uniquely good in
each detail, lends distinction to ('crowns') the deed itself
('what you are doing'), so that all your acts are pre-
eminent' – the deed, itself indifferent, is dignified by the
performer. Or we may perhaps say: 'Your performance
of it ('each your doing'), uniquely good in each detail,
makes superior ('crowns') whatever you may be doing
at present ('in the present deeds'), so that all your acts are
(successively) pre-eminent'. In this interpretation the lover
sees his mistress' deeds as a scale of rising perfections.
Thirdly, we may say with less strain than in the corresponding interpretation of the first two lines: 'Your performance
of it, uniquely good in each detail, renders superior what
you are doing, among the deeds of all present ('present
deeds' being now understood as a reference to place
and not time), so that all your acts are pre-eminent'.
There is no reason to regard the speech as in any way
corrupt. It is not necessary for a passage of verse to
bear only one clearly defined prose meaning; in poetry
ambiguity is a form of compression – several meanings
are suggested in one packed phrase. Even though Shakespeare, we are told, may have borrowed the conceit in
Florizel's speech from Sidney's *Arcadia*,[1] it is likely that
he would add a complexity which is not to be found
in the original. I do not, of course, suggest that the
strands of meaning which I have laboriously teased

[1] *V. Arden Shakespeare*, p. 78.

out were at all clearly differentiated in his own mind.[1]

Returning to our exegesis, 'crowns' and 'queens' relate directly to Perdita's 'May Queen' costume but also hint at her true origin and destiny and associate her as life-symbol with the divine gift of royalty. There is nothing in the speech that applies particularly to the speaker himself except the general and obvious suggestion that he is in love. Perhaps also the quality of his love may be indicated; the tough thinking suggests a deeper and more firmly rooted passion than Romeo's, for instance. What the verse conveys in addition to the lover's speech in its surface meaning and emotional quality is not information about the character of Florizel, which we should expect in a naturalistic play, but, as we have seen, a number of inter-linked attitudes not conceived of as in the mind of Florizel at all – attitudes related to the love theme yet contributing to a meaning within and below the surface events of the play. The tenseness of rhythm and complex thought are no indication of Florizel's intellectual qualities; they are the direct expression of Shakespeare's complex and pro-found reading of experience. Even lovers' speeches must do more than merely echo the natural lovers' sentiment; they must present this sentiment, but analysed and related to the general theme. Characters thus tend to say more

---

[1] Furness in *The Variorum Shakespeare* (p. 202), after quoting the comments of other critics on the concluding lines of Florizel's speech, follows with his own note: 'Whatever difficulty there is in this passage lies in the phrase "in the present deeds". It does not seem to have occurred to any of the critics that in those words Florizel is referring to Perdita's present distribution of flowers and to her bearing towards her guests. Had the phrase been "at the present time", which is, I think, its equivalent in meaning, no one, I suppose, would have deemed the sentence corrupt or mutilated. The whole sentence may be paraphrased: Your way of doing everything (so peculiarly your own in every particular) crowns what you are at present doing, so that all your acts are queens'.' The apostrophe in 'queens'', if intentional, is rather a prosaic reduction of the meaning, but as Furness makes no comment on the matter here and below objects to Singer's reading of 'queen's', also without further comment, I incline to regard it as a misprint – or it may be a quotation mark, in which case the misprint occurs above in the omission of a corresponding quotation mark to open the paraphrase. The *Arden* edition in quoting the paraphrase silently omits this baffling punctuation. In general, Furness' interpretation is not unlike my own first paraphrase above.

than is necessary for the conduct of the action, yet with an
air of urgent relevancy, so that the verse itself invites
attention to themes not explicitly stated. This is true of the
Florizel speech we have considered and of Polixenes'
speech in the same scene, in which he pleads that the
gardener's art is a part of nature:

> . . . nature is made better by no mean
> But nature makes that mean: so, over that art
> Which you say adds to nature, is an art
> That nature makes. You see, sweet maid, we marry
> A gentler scion to the wildest stock,
> And make conceive a bark of baser kind
> By bud of nobler race: this is an art
> Which does mend nature, change it rather, but
> The art itself is nature.   (IV. iv. 89)

Although on the story level Perdita remains unconvinced,
the serious presentation of the argument commends it to
our notice. Superficially it is an excuse for gillyvors and
grafting; it is also ironic, as Polixenes is soon to object to
the marriage of the gentle scion, his son, with Perdita's
supposedly wilder stock. But there is a further application.
This generalisation about Art and Nature is placed cen-
trally in the development of the spring theme and put
into the mouth of the most illustrious representative of the
court. Does it not, then, hint at the opposition of court
and country which Shakespeare has had in mind since
As You Like It, suggesting that a worthy culture must con-
sist in the marriage of urban and rural virtues and that
that aspect of civilisation which 'mends' or improves our
natural condition – not distorts it, as evil does – is itself
part of the natural order?

This examination of the verse has provided data which
I shall use at succeeding stages of my argument. At the
outset it is clear that there is no flagging in Shakespeare's
poetic energy and that, however marvellous and remote
the story, we are presented in the verse with a lively intellectual treatment of contemporary life and contemporary

issues. This is indicated not only by the imagery but by the physical properties of the verse; its varied and contorted rhythms, its stress and strain, suggest an energetic confronting of reality, even in the most Arcadian setting. It is interesting to compare the verse of Fletcher's *Faithful Shepherdess*, which is almost contemporary with *The Winter's Tale*; it was first produced probably in 1609 or 1610 and *The Winter's Tale* probably in 1611.[1] In Fletcher the imagery itself is deliberately Arcadian, remote from everyday affairs, and the verse flows in smooth, seductively melodious lines:

> Oh, you are fairer far
> Than the chaste blushing morn, or that fair star
> That guides the wandering seaman through the deep;
> Straighter than the straightest pine upon the steep
> Head of an aged mountain, and more white
> Than the new milk we strip before day-light
> From the full-freighted bags of our fair flocks;
> Your hair more beauteous than those hanging locks
> Of young Apollo! (I. ii. 61)

The 'propriety' of imagery is a new sophistication; Perdita's white hand, we remember, was like an Ethiopian's tooth, but Fletcher limits himself to expressions which would be possible in the mouth of that impossible figure, the Arcadian shepherd. It is a step nearer naturalism, but in an Arcadian play it is a very long step away from serious concern with the contemporary world. The praise of chastity, which is the play's apparent theme, is presented with an equally sophisticated distrust of natural feeling. *The Faithful Shepherdess* is a pleasant enough play but it is distinctly light entertainment, 'escape' for the world-weary courtier of King James. If in writing *The Winter's Tale* Shakespeare had Beaumont and Fletcher in mind at all, we must see in the astringency of his verse not a conscious imitation but a deliberate criticism and challenge.

[1] Authorities seem generally to agree on 1611 as the probable date of *The Winter's Tale*. Mr. W. W. Greg suggests 'a hypothetical 1609' for *The Faithful Shepherdess; v. The Works of Francis Beaumont and John Fletcher, Variorum Edition* (George Bell & Sons and A. H. Bullen, 1908), Vol. III, p. 3.

III – 'AN OLD TALE'

WHY, THEN, did Shakespeare choose something so remote from contemporary life as this tale of wonder and adventure in the old Hellenic world, if he had no desire to escape the pressure of his own times? There is the matter of popularity; Arcadia had been established in fashionable circles by the energies of Sir Philip Sidney and popularised in such works as Greene's *Pandosto*, on which *The Winter's Tale* is founded. A succession of tales and plays and masques sustained the Golden Age into the reign of King James, while a new quality of romantic impossibility was infused into the drama by Beaumont and Fletcher, though not many of their successes of this type seem to have been produced before the period of Shakespeare's romances. Shakespeare himself had made his modest fortune and retired to Stratford; he was writing infrequently and presumably because he wanted to write. As a practical man of the theatre and an investor in theatrical enterprises, he would hardly be indifferent to box-office considerations, but there is no reason to believe him to have been dominated by them. He may have derived an ironic pleasure from taking a fashionable literary mode, as he does here, and subjecting it to a sea-change. But, though he might enjoy unclassical variations on a pastoral theme, there is a seriousness in the poetry which forbids us to regard this as his main object. We are forced to conclude that he chose this naïve story because it best suited his (perhaps unconscious) purposes. He must indeed have found it fascinating, for he chooses substantially the same story from *Pericles* to *The Tempest*.

The Winter's Tale is 'an old tale'. The oracle motive with its accompaniment of strange adventure goes back to pre-Christian Greece[1] in a literary tradition covering two

---

[1] *V. Arden Shakespeare*, Introduction, pp. xix *et seq.*

millenia and its oral tradition may go back centuries before; it certainly has all the marks of 'folk' origin (whatever that may mean) with its suggestion of parable and a possible religious significance. The whole tale is one of marvels, of the supernatural and the miraculous. Jealousy comes apparently unmotivated and unprompted to Leontes, his son pines mysteriously away, his daughter is strangely lost and strangely found, the severed friendships of Sicilia and Bohemia are thus remarkably renewed and Hermione comes back again as from the dead. The pronouncement of the oracle is central in position and significance and its fulfilment marks the *dénouement* of the play. Shakespeare had always favoured old tales – the venerable casket story and the tale of Lear – and he seems rather to have approved the 'improbabilities' which psychologists have found so disturbing. His universe was not the neatly depressing universe of psychological determinism; he found room for the two poles of natural and supernatural between which humanity is poised; for providence and guidance, miracle, mysterious prompting to good or evil – a whole range of inexplicable experience over against, yet intimately bound up with, the natural affections, social sanctions and other manifestations of the natural order. *The Winter's Tale* expresses this universe more clearly than would a story derived from contemporary Jacobean life, since it makes obvious on the plane of recognisable events what is usually concealed by the familiarity of routine existence. The hand of Providence is easier to trace in the marvellous happenings of a remote time than in the less spectacular lives of our neighbours.

Fairy tales, romance and adventure appeal to us, not just because they are different from our ordinary experience but because they present in easily assimilable form an essential element of that experience, the shrouding mystery of life and the tremulous human desire for an unseen glory. Wordsworth and others have been able to express directly something of this mystery in common things, but Shakespeare, concerned with a theatre audience, chose a remote setting, distancing and simplifying the miraculous yet bringing it home by the strictly contemporary quality of his verse. At first sight this may seem a cruder method, but it is in fact more subtle and, indeed, more than a method. In looking back to remote and simpler times, Shakespeare shares a common poetic attitude: classical and renaissance poets recalled the Golden Age; Herbert and Vaughan looked back to the patriarchs and beyond them to Eden and the innocent childhood-state when man walked close with God. And, behind the professed poets, the submerged poetry in every man has striven through myth and legend to recreate a vanished blessedness which faintly survives in the unconscious memory of the race. This is one strain in the complex harmony of *The Winter's Tale*; it is seen especially in the sinless sensuality of Perdita, who is more truly representative of the age of innocence than Milton's Eve. In contrast we have Leontes' jealousy, the spider in the cup, and the fallen sophistication of contemporary life. But the guilty are redeemed by the innocent, the gods overrule all things and the final victory is theirs. Thus Shakespeare fuses the remote and the familiar, the ancient and the modern, in a statement of eternal truth transcending time and place; *The Winter's Tale* is an attempt more successful than that of James Joyce to put 'Allspace in a Notshall'.[1] The world of romance lies beyond space and time; in Arcadia we may expect 'poetic justice' and to see clearly what our own world presents in a glass darkly. And so the beneficent ordering of the universe, imperfectly discerned on the terrestrial plane and only properly fulfilled in eternity, may be presented in terms of an earthly life freed from historical limitations yet rendered contemporary by the living idiom of the poetry in which it is expressed.

---

[1] *Finnegans Wake* (Faber and Faber, 1939), p. 455. Joyce uses the phrase to describe eternity, but it seems applicable also to his own artistic purpose.

IV – PLACE AND TIME

'THE SEA-COAST of Bohemia' has been much debated ever since Ben Jonson drew the attention of William Drummond of Hawthornden to Shakespeare's apparent blunder. The usual opinion seems to be that Greene perpetrated a geographical howler and Shakespeare copied, like a bad boy in the examination room. I do not claim a Scriptural inerrancy for Shakespeare's plays but I do believe a certain humility to be necessary in Shakespearean criticism; Shakespeare is less likely than I am to be wrong. But, even if Shakespeare were an illiterate from the Stratfordian backwoods, we must remember that Greene had a university education and, though geography was not in the recognised curriculum of those dark days, when people were expected to travel for such information, it may well be supposed that he would have some acquaintance with the map of Europe. Furness, in *The Variorum Shakespeare*[1], seems to accept the explanation of an anonymous writer in the early nineteenth century that Bohemia did at one time have access to the sea, but as this was *circa* 1270, I do not think it any injustice to Greene and Shakespeare to question their knowledge of this obscure matter of history. We can also ignore the discovery of Dr. von Lippmann that in 1481 the name 'Bohemia' was used of Apulia, since even in the text where he finds this usage[2] a note of explanation is given, so that the fact cannot have been widely known. Much more important is a passage in the autobiography of Lord Herbert of Cherbury which, on first reading it, I felt cast an entirely new light on the matter. I find that it has not escaped previous commentators; it is mentioned by Farmer,[3] and Sir Sidney Lee, the editor of

[1] Preface, p. ix; also pp. 139 *et seq*.
[2] Tschamser's *Annals of the Bare-footed Friars of Thann; v. Variorum Shakespeare*, p. 141.
[3] *V. Variorum Shakespeare*, p. 140.

the autobiography, draws attention to the Shakespearean
parallel,[1] but neither has any useful comment to make
upon it. Lord Herbert, who is conceited and entirely
humourless, writes of 'one Monsieur de Luynes', a favourite
and adviser of Louis XIII of France: 'How unfit this man
was for the credit he had with the King may be argued by
this; that when there was question made about some
business in Bohemia, he demanded whether it was an
inland country, or lay upon the sea?'[2] It seems rather
curious that an English romance-writer and a French
diplomat should make the same error and that Shakespeare, remarkable for his various knowledge, should complete this ill-assorted trio of dunces. From the tone of
Lord Herbert and the probability that he had gained his
knowledge of de Luynes' supposed blunder from courtiers'
gossip, it would appear that the generality of folk were
quite clear that Bohemia had no coastline; otherwise the
story would hardly have gained currency or be used by
Lord Herbert as an illustration of de Luynes' unfitness for
his post. Then, if everybody was familiar with this item of
geographical knowledge, does it not seem likely that Greene
and Shakespeare and de Luynes himself would be no
exceptions to the rule? What I suspect is one of those
'chestnuts' surviving many decades and told and re-told
in various company – an old joke of international reputation, intercourse with the Continent being closer in those
days. A modern parallel to the sea-coast of Bohemia would
be the Swiss navy or Wigan pier. Such a joke might well
become attached to a French diplomat who was something
of a buffoon, as in a university to-day a good story will
tend to attach itself to a suitable professorial figure and a
very good story may survive several generations of dons,
being told circumstantially of a particular victim in each
generation. Lord Herbert is just the type who would

---

[1] *The Autobiography of Edward, Lord Herbert of Cherbury*, with Introduction,
etc., by Sidney Lee, *Second Edition, Revised* (George Routledge & Sons, no
date), p. 105.
[2] *Op. cit.*, pp. 104-105.

C

fail to see the joke and so record it as serious history.

This view of the matter is further supported by a passage in Taylor, the Water-poet, quoted by Collier.[1] Taylor had visited Prague in 1620 and on his return wrote an account of his journey. In his address to the reader he ridicules the ignorance of the London aldermen: 'I am no sooner eased of him, but Gregory Gandergoose, an Alderman of Gotham, catches me by the goll, demanding if Bohemia be a great town, whether there be any meat in it, and whether the last fleet of ships be arrived there'. Collier uses this to illustrate the geographical ignorance of Shakespeare's contemporaries and so misses the real point. For Taylor, though writing for a popular audience, certainly expected his readers to know more about Bohemia than did Gregory Gandergoose, since if they did not know that Bohemia had no sea-coast his satire would have fallen flat. It is remarkable that this obvious point should have escaped Collier himself, Furness who quotes his note, and other commentators who must have read it. Why, then, should Taylor count on his readers' possession of this obscure piece of geographical information? Even the marriage of the Princess Elizabeth to the ill-fated Winter King would hardly produce a national interest in Bohemian geography. Surely the only explanation is that the sea-coast of Bohemia was already a stock joke on which Taylor was merely ringing the changes. For a writer a reference to Bohemia with its well-known non-existent coastline might thus be a useful indication of the degree of credibility to attach to a story in which it occurred. I suggest that Greene insisted on Bohemia's coastline to emphasise the fact that his Bohemia was not the Bohemia of contemporary diplomatic reports but a romantic Ruritania or Arcadia where the strangest things might happen. And Shakespeare, who rejected so much of Greene's story in adapting it to his purpose, deliberately preserved the sea-coast of Bohemia because he was especially anxious to liberate

[1] *V. Variorum Shakespeare*, p. 140.

himself from the localisation of his play world in the contemporary map of Europe. In more recent times a writer
such as W. S. Gilbert might well have presented us with an
admiral in the Swiss navy and from such indications a
Savoy audience would gauge the degree of reality to be
attributed to his plot. It is a great pity that critics of
Shakespeare cannot be brought to think of some matters
in terms of the Savoyards.

Here, then, is a warning that we are not to take our
geography too seriously; we may compare Prospero's
island, which is presumably somewhere in the Mediterranean, although most of its attributes seem to be taken
from accounts of West Indian voyages. Apart from the sea-
coast we are told nothing of Bohemia – or of Sicilia.
Tinkler contrasts the urbanised Sicilia with pastoral
Bohemia on the strength of an alleged sophistication at
the court of Sicily and a sheep-shearing feast somewhere in
Bohemia, but Autolycus satirises the Bohemian courtiers
as if they had all the Jacobean sophistications and, though
Leontes himself has the failings of sophistication in his
torturing jealousy, there is an uncouth honesty in the way
Paulina and his courtiers 'answer back' and make almost
a figure of fun out of the poor, persecuted tyrant who
cannot even kill his wife's child without raising a storm of
protest.

Time is a more subtle and important factor. Shakespeare
had always been concerned with the problem of time and
in *The Winter's Tale* the sixteen years between Act III and
Act IV are bridged by 'Time, the Chorus':

> . . . it is in my power
> To o'erthrow law and in one self-born hour
> To plant and o'erwhelm custom. Let me pass
> The same I am, ere ancient'st order was
> Or what is now received: I witness to
> The times that brought them in; so shall I do
> To the freshest things now reigning and make stale
> The glistering of this present, as my tale
> Now seems to it.   (IV. i. 7)

Time is himself timeless, outside the changing process of history; he serves to remind us directly of the interest of such an old tale to ourselves, for 'the glistering of this present' shall become an old tale to future ages, while Time himself shall remain unchanged. Here is a direct statement of what is implied in contrasting the old tale and the contemporary verse; it is a strange conjuring with reality, for the audience, having preened themselves on their superiority to these creatures of a vague and distant past, are momentarily jolted into seeing themselves from the same viewpoint, looking back at themselves from a remote future as down the wrong end of a telescope. Time the Chorus not only spans the sixteen years between two halves of the story but also in a few lines of poetry transcends the contrast of past and present, climbs above time, and at the same time closely involves the audience in a timeless drama.[1]

So-called anachronism also helps to produce an impression of timeless universality. A notorious instance is the reference to Julio Romano, in Act v, Scene ii. The only reason for selecting a famous sculptor of the Italian Renaissance as the artist responsible for the supposed statue of Hermione must have been the very fact of his fame. The 'Third Gentleman' accounts for the 'statue's' lifelike resemblance to Hermione by ascribing it to Julio Romano, and there would be no point in this if Shakespeare had not assumed that Romano would be known, at least to the educated members of his audience, as either a great sculptor or a sculptor of lifelike portraits. Yet, if the audience knew so much, they would presumably be aware that he belonged to the Renaissance, not the Graeco-Roman period; indeed, he is referred to as 'that rare Italian

---

[1] Professor Dover Wilson, in the *New Cambridge Shakespeare* (p. 159), considers this speech of Time to be the work of a 'collaborator' and complains of 'its forced rhymes, its jerky rhythms and its obscure emptiness'. An unenterprising smoothness of rhyme and rhythm is more likely to suggest the hack writer, and the passage, though somewhat obscure at a first reading, is so far from empty that it carefully sums up all that Shakespeare is doing with the time theme in the play as a whole.

master' (v. ii. 105), a phrase which seems almost designed
to draw the audience's attention to this outstanding
anachronism. It would have been easy enough to name a
Greek sculptor instead, especially as the Pygmalion story
was well known in Marston's version and has such obvious
affinity with the 'coming alive' of Hermione, but Shakespeare sacrificed here an interesting and involved reference
which must surely have been in his thoughts. Anachronism
such as this is clearly not due to the writer's ignorance; in a
sense it is quite deliberate. But it is not self-conscious,
since there is no evidence that Shakespeare ever considered
the alternative of writing in historical perspective. Moreover, I do not for a moment believe that he had any
conscious intention of using such means to 'transcend
history'; this is merely their unconscious effect.[1] Similarly
though less obviously anachronistic is Hermione's passing
reference to her father as the Emperor of Russia (III. ii. 120),
which even to a Jacobean audience must momentarily
have suggested an atmosphere very different from the
Mediterranean world of classical antiquity familiar to
them through their ordinary grammar-school education.

Mr. Moorman, editing the *Arden* edition of *The Winter's
Tale*, comments upon the care with which Shakespeare
has evoked 'the religious atmosphere of classical Greece'.
'No Christian sentiment,' he says, 'is permitted to fall from
the lips of any of the characters in the stress of the conflict
to which they are subjected. It is Jove and the "good goddess Nature" that Paulina invokes in order that Hermione's
child may be saved from the yellow taint of jealousy,'
etc.[2] I should myself regard the religious atmosphere as
emphatically Christian, while the pagan suggestions give
authenticity to the story and serve to 'distance' the
Christian attitudes, presenting them in a new setting so as

[1] For a fuller treatment of this subject see the chapter 'Anachronism and
the Treatment of Time' in my *Shakespeare and the Popular Dramatic Tradition*,
pp. 42 *et seq.*
[2] *Op. cit.*, Introduction, p. xxiii. This passage is quoted approvingly in the
New Cambridge Shakespeare, Introduction, p. xvi.

to counteract the deadening influence of familiarity and escape the deadly influence of contemporary controversy over minor theological questions. The oracle, which is central to the working out both of the plot and of the play's deeper significance, is admittedly the oracle of Apollo; and Hermione's piety is ostensibly pagan: 'Apollo be my judge!' (III. ii. 117). Other pagan deities are sometimes mentioned, especially by Perdita in the distribution of flowers, where the religious significance of spring, not peculiar to paganism, is naturally expressed in pagan terms:

> O Proserpina,
> For the flowers now, that frighted thou let'st fall
> From Dis's waggon! daffodils,
> That come before the swallow dares, and take
> The winds of March with beauty; violets dim,
> But sweeter than the lids of Juno's eyes
> Or Cytherea's breath; pale primroses,
> That die unmarried, ere they can behold
> Bright Phœbus in his strength.   (IV. iv. 116)

Yet Perdita herself goes on to compare this 'pagan' ceremonial with a Christian observance:

> Methinks I play as I have seen them do
> In Whitsun pastorals.   (IV. iv. 133)

The play, in fact, has as many obviously Christian references as pagan. The doctrine of original sin appears early in the second scene of Act I; Polixenes and Leontes had been innocent in boyhood:

> Had we pursued that life,
> And our weak spirits ne'er been higher rear'd
> With stronger blood, we should have answer'd heaven
> Boldly 'not guilty'; the imposition clear'd
> Hereditary ours.   (I. ii. 71)

Hermione's 'Grace to boot!' (I. ii. 80) is shortly followed by a passage which I do not wholly understand:

> My last good deed was to entreat his stay:
> What was my first? it has an elder sister,
> Or I mistake you: O, would her name were Grace!
>   (I. ii. 97)

It seems likely that in the last phrase there is a pun upon 'Grace' as a Christian name and as a term in Christian theology and that in these two references a major theme has been casually introduced. Neither playwright nor audience need have been fully aware of this, but the doctrine of grace was so widely discussed in sixteenth- and seventeenth-century theology, even in the most popular sermons and lectures, that the repetition of the term may well have set up in the audience a receptiveness to theological implications. After Leontes' reply Hermione exclaims "'Tis grace indeed' (I. ii. 105). At the end of the same scene Polixenes refers to Judas Iscariot. If he has 'touched the queen forbiddenly':

> O, then my best blood turn
> To an infected jelly and my name
> Be yoked with his that did betray the Best!   (I. ii. 417)

The implied comparison between Hermione and Our Lord is interesting. As she is borne to prison she says:

> . . . this action I now go on
> Is for my better grace –   (II. i. 121)

and the word here may signify more than the 'reputation, credit' of the *New Cambridge Shakespeare's* glossary. Hermione's attitude to the pagan gods is in fact Christian, not pagan; she is not unlike the medieval 'patient Griselda' but with a dignity and fire which the Middle Ages would scarcely have approved, though it is compatible with humility and the desire for 'pity, not revenge' (III. ii. 124). The piety of other characters is often consistent with either pagan or Christian religion, as in Antigonus' submission to the gods – 'Their sacred wills be done!' (III. iii. 8) – but the old Shepherd, as we have seen, knew the minor ceremonies of Christian burial. The importance attached to moral attitudes is especially Christian; in Greek tragedy it is the deed that matters, even if innocently done, but Leontes suffers as much for what he thought of doing as for

what he actually did. Also his penance, in itself indiffer-
ently pagan or Christian, has been performed in Christian
penitence; he has

> . . . perform'd
> A saint-like sorrow.   (v. i. 1)

Paulina, again, may speak of 'the gods' but the asceticism
she deems inadequate is hardly Greek:

> A thousand knees
> Ten thousand years together, naked, fasting,
> Upon a barren mountain, and still winter
> In storm perpetual, could not move the gods
> To look that way thou wert.   (III. ii. 211)

In an earlier scene, when Leontes threatens 'I'll ha' thee
burnt', she replies:

> I care not:
> It is an heretic that makes the fire,
> Not she which burns in't.   (II. iii. 114)

I cannot agree with Hudson[1] that Shakespeare is here
taking a strong line against ecclesiastical tyranny; the use
of 'an' and 'she' instead of 'the' and 'he' shows that he is
not generalising one way or another. Paulina is thinking
only of the immediate case; Leontes is a heretic about
Hermione, and Paulina herself a true believer. In any
event the reference is a long way from the Hellenic world.
Perhaps we have already sufficiently established the
presence of 'Christian sentiments' in the play. Many more
such passages will be considered in Part Two, when we
come to the question of interpretation.

The conflation of past and present may be observed in
the secular as well as the religious life portrayed in *The
Winter's Tale*. There is a general feeling of remote antiquity
in the naïveté of the story and the insistence that it is 'an
old tale'. The court life of Sicilia is simple, not to say crude
(despite a parallel suggestion of over-sophistication), and
in Bohemia a king and his minister may dog the

[1] *V. Variorum Shakespeare*, p. 107.

crown prince to a sheep-shearing feast. On the other
hand, there is an abundant presentation of contemporary
Jacobean life. Apart from 'having served Prince Florizel
and in his time worn three-pile' (IV. iii. 13), Autolycus,
as itinerant pedlar, ballad-monger, cozener and cut-purse,
might come straight out of Thomas Harman's *A Caveat
for Cursetors:*[1]

> A wild Rogue is he that is born a Rogue, he is more subtle and more
> given by nature to all kind of knavery than the other, as beastly
> begotten in barn or bushes, and from his infancy traded up in
> treachery: yea and before ripeness of years doth permit wallowing
> in lewd lechery, but that is counted amongst them no sin.[2]

His means of procuring a living are no more varied and
ingenious than those recorded in Harman and the 'coney-
catching' literature, and his ballads, however remarkable,
are not exorbitant in their burlesque of popular Jacobean
broadsides:

> Here's one to a very doleful tune, how a usurer's wife was brought
> to bed of twenty money-bags at a burthen and how she longed
> to eat adders' heads and toads carbonadoed.   (IV. iv. 265)

The satire against courtiers is also typically Jacobean and
Autolycus again is the chief instrument of this criticism of
the court:

> Whether it like me or no, I am a courtier. Seest thou not the air
> of the court in these enfoldings? hath not my gait in it the measure
> of the court? receives not thy nose court-odour from me? reflect
> I not on thy baseness court-contempt? Thinkest thou, for that I
> insinuate, or toaze from thee thy business, I am therefore no courtier?
> I am courtier cap-a-pe . . .   (IV. iv. 754)

The repetition of 'court' and 'courtier' gives a satiric bite
to the fustian of comedy. In Act v, Scene ii, we have

---

[1] Reprinted in *The Old Book Collector's Miscellany*, ed. Charles Hindley
(Reeves and Turner, 1871), Vol. I.
[2] *Op. cit.*, Cap. V, p. 38.

Shakespeare's last burlesque of court jargon; the gentlemen are discussing Perdita's meeting with Leontes after
her recognition as his daughter:

> One of the prettiest touches of all and that which angled for mine
> eyes, caught the water though not the fish, was when, at the relation
> of the queen's death, with the manner how she came to't bravely
> confessed and lamented by the king, how attentiveness wounded
> his daughter; till, from one sign of dolour to another, she did, with
> an 'Alas', I would fain say, bleed tears, for I am sure my heart
> wept blood.   (v. ii. 89)

This can only be burlesque; Shakespeare had always
enjoyed a thrust at such affectation, and a straight line
runs from Don Armado through Osric to these gentlemen
in *The Winter's Tale*.

The Bohemian rustics are notably Elizabethan – or
Jacobean – and the sheep-shearing feast, 'romantic' in outline and sometimes pagan in detail, is taken in the main
from the Warwickshire countryside to which Shakespeare
had recently returned. These slow-thinking country folk
who flock about the pedlar, eager for his wares and so
easily 'taken in', are interested above all in his ballads,
because they tell of life in the great city. There is the
tendency – not quite vanished even to-day – to regard
everything as true which finds its way into print: 'I love
a ballad in print o' life, for then we are sure they are true'
(IV. iv. 263). Perhaps this hints at the deleterious effect
upon rural life of 'these most brisk and giddy-paced times'
(*Twelfth Night*, II. iv. 6). The contemporary skill in music is
faithfully reflected; on this theme even Mopsa can speak
with easy assurance: 'We can both sing it: if thou'lt bear a
part, thou shalt hear; 'tis in three parts' (IV. iv. 298). There
are healthy local touches even about the food: 'saffron to
colour the warden pies' (IV. iii. 48) could be a dominant
interest only in the England of Elizabeth and the early
Stuarts – with the Hanoverians we move on to beef and
beer. The time factor is further complicated by the fact
that even within this contemporary rustic world there are

two contrasting generations. The old Shepherd has a certain dignity which never deserts him and which contrasts strongly with the clownishness of his son, called significantly 'Clown' in the *dramatis personæ*. When they come into good fortune, the son, claiming to be 'a gentleman born' (v. ii. 145), shows himself a swaggering upstart, but the old man has the elements of true gentility: 'we must be gentle, now we are gentlemen' (v. ii. 164).[1] The old Shepherd survives from an age when the fields and the farm provided a worthy and dignified life-work; his description of his 'old wife' looks back regretfully to the old days:

> Fie, daughter! when my old wife lived, upon
> This day she was both pantler, butler, cook,
> Both dame and servant; welcomed all, served all;
> Would sing her song and dance her turn; now here,
> At upper end o' the table, now i' the middle;
> On his shoulder, and his; her face o' fire
> With labour and the thing she took to quench it,
> She would to each one sip. You are retired,
> As if you were a feasted one and not
> The hostess of the meeting . . .   (IV. iv. 55)

The contrast with Perdita not only brings out the disabilities of royal birth; it is also another aspect of the contrast between older and younger generations; the old Shepherd presumably suspects Perdita of scorning the menial tasks which his own 'old wife' had been content to perform. The influence of town ways was reaching the country by other and more insidious means than the pedlar's pack. Shakespeare in his lifetime saw the effects of enclosure and the exploitation of the countryside on a capitalistic scale by commercial speculators from the city; the older generation remembered its feudal loyalties but a younger generation grew up knowing only the ways of the city landlords. *The Winter's Tale* conveys Shakespeare's mature reflection upon this social problem which he had

---

[1] Tinkler makes this point; *loc. cit.*, p. 351.

treated years before in *As You Like It*, where Corin complains of his 'churlish' master who

> . . . little recks to find the way to heaven
> By doing deeds of hospitality.[1]   (II. iv. 81)

Thus in Shakespeare's treatment of the time factor the audience is made aware (*a*) of a contrast between the remote ancient world of the story and the contemporary world of the rustics, the court-satire and the verse, and (*b*) of a contrast between two generations in the contemporary world. Out of this apparent confusion of times the timeless world of romance is created and the action appropriately distanced for detached criticism, while contemporary references and the nature of the verse insist on the play's immediate relation to the contemporary world. Moreover, this is not only a means of arousing in the audience a certain quality of attention; it also constitutes a statement about the nature of the universe, one of the many interlocking statements which make up the poetic content of the play. We are made to appreciate the significance of time and change – the power which can transmute this living present into an old tale of shadowy recollection – and to perceive at the same time, beyond time, a changeless divine order whose redemptive function is providentially effective within the time-process; for the story of Leontes has been placed outside time to ensure its universal application.

V – THE MEANING OF A SONG

THE JUXTAPOSITION of the timeless world of romance and the contemporary scene brings us also to realise that the essential qualities of the former, its mystery and beauty, are qualities discoverable in the most intractable material of our own times. This is perhaps most completely conveyed in a lyric of Autolycus; it is characteristic of Shakespeare

[1] *V. Shakespeare and the Popular Dramatic Tradition*, Ch. V, pp. 95-96.

that the very songs, introduced apparently haphazard,
should reveal layers of deep meaning – perhaps deeper
than his own conscious intention:

> When daffodils begin to peer,
> With heigh! the doxy over the dale,
> Why, then comes in the sweet o' the year;
> For the red blood reigns in the winter's pale.
>
> The white sheet bleaching on the hedge,
> With heigh! the sweet birds, O, how they sing!
> Doth set my pugging tooth on edge;
> For a quart of ale is a dish for a king.
>
> The lark, that tirra-lyra chants,
> With heigh! with heigh! the thrush and the jay,
> Are summer songs for me and my aunts,
> While we lie tumbling in the hay.   (IV. iii. 1)

In rhythm and metre this is just another pleasant Elizabethan lyric, rather out of period in Jacobean times; its
simplicity and traditional character are avouched in the
'heigh' of each second line, the monosyllabic language, the
sparing use of epithets, and a Chaucerian phrase, 'the
sweet birds, O, how they sing!'[1] Yet the song is startling
enough, as studiously different from its Elizabethan pro-
genitors as Donne's innocent-seeming 'Come live with me
and be my love' from Marlowe's original. Donne's are
'new pleasures' and so are Shakespeare's, for the song contrasts the poet's countryside with the 'low life' of the
organised thieves, who in those times formed a community of outcasts with their own language and customs
and their own unelevated morals. We begin with the
daffodils, but the alliterative 'doxy' in the second line
signifies one of the women held in common among the
community of thieves. 'Winter's pale', we may note in
passing, supplies a pun on 'pale' meaning 'boundary' and
'pale' in colouring, from the absence of sun. The white
sheet on the hedge suggests the decent activity of cottage
and farm, but a 'pugging tooth', on the analogy of a

---

[1] Cf. *Nonne Preestes Tale*, l. 381: 'Herkneth thise blisful briddes how they singe'.

'sweet tooth', means a thievish tooth,[1] a desire to steal in
order to purchase the quart of ale which, though a dish
for a king, is obtained by means that the king would hardly
approve. In the third stanza we begin innocently again
with the bird-songs, lark and thrush and jay, but 'aunts'
are women of loose morals, paramours – in this instance
presumably doxies. If 'doxy' and 'aunts' and the third line
of the second stanza had been replaced by something
pleasantly innocuous, then the whole song would be passed
without comment. As it is we have a curious drawing
together of quite different types of experience. Elizabethan
and Jacobean authors wrote up 'low life' with as much
gusto as a certain school of novelists do to-day; and the
Elizabethan 'nature lyric' is well known. Only in the song
of Autolycus, however, do these strands of interest inter-
weave and produce a metaphysical lyric of wide significance. I do not regard it as justifying the ill ways of Autolycus; but it is concerned with metaphysics, not morals.
Its primary importance is in bringing the ideal world of
romance into unmistakable relation with contemporary
life, even in its less savoury aspects – all life, however de-
praved, is shot through with the divine reality symbolised
in the 'romance' and expressed here in terms of natural
beauty. The Victorians accorded this song a 'single mixed
response', as Miss Bradbrook would say,[2] and saw Autolycus as 'a good fellow', a 'knight of the road', no doubt with
a heart of gold. In reality the type was no pleasanter than
the modern petty thief and 'confidence man'. What
Shakespeare supplies is a juxtaposition of opposites, an
association of natural beauty with the nasty sneak-thief
and his unlovely companions. As a character, Autolycus
who can 'sleep out the thought' of the life to come[3] (IV.
iii. 31), is shown to have saving graces, and his song
expresses this same truth in metaphysical poetry where

---

[1] Probably again with a pun on 'pug-tooth' meaning 'eye tooth', a form
found in the Devonshire dialect; v. Arden Shakespeare, pp. 66-67.

[2] V. Elizabethan Stage Conditions (C.U.P., 1932), p. 93.

[3] V. Appendix B.

religious vision penetrates beyond the over-simplified moral
judgment of the world. That this is a comic song – for the
unexpectedness of 'doxy' in the second line, for instance,
is surely comic – only gives stability to the serious theme.
Shakespeare's is not an easy optimism – the daffodil and
the doxy are contrasted not complementary – but his
clear sight perceives the sun which shines alike on the just
and the unjust[1] and there is therefore nothing magisterial
in his judgments.

VI – ANTIQUATED TECHNIQUE AND THE PLANES OF REALITY

IT WOULD seem that Shakespeare's artistic judgment served
him well in choosing an ancient and naïve story to carry
the burden of his deepest thought, but the question still
remains: Why is his dramatic technique crude and apparently incoherent? The technique of *The Winter's Tale* is
commonly regarded as deficient on a number of counts.
First there is that awkward gap of sixteen years between
the two parts of the play. This we may justify as providing
necessary material for the complex statement about time;
it must have been deliberate, for *The Tempest* seems
deliberately and mockingly to repudiate the suggestion
that Shakespeare was incapable of preserving the unities
when he wanted to. The introduction of new characters
half-way through the play and the abandoning of the
principal character for so long a time are faults in con-
struction only if the play is to be regarded as primarily
psychological, a study in the development of character.
To begin with a preconceived notion of the nature of a
play and criticise any failure to fulfil its requirements is

[1] There is a direct reminiscence of this Scriptural phrase in Perdita's remark
later:

> The selfsame sun that shines upon his court
> Hides not his visage from our cottage but
> Looks on alike.   (IV. iv. 455)

surely apriorism of the wrong kind; the fact that Shakespeare does treat characters somewhat cavalierly must be
taken as an indication that he has other dramatic fish to
fry. This would explain the notoriously unmotivated
jealousy of Leontes (though I shall suggest that it has a
further significance), the casual disposal of Antigonus
(*Exit, pursued by a bear*) and the rather tenuous charac-
terisation of every one save Leontes in his jealousy.

The stagecraft is justifiably described as crude or naïve.
We have the frequently remarked *Exit, pursued by a bear*,
and there is a patch of astonishingly awkward management
towards the end of Act IV, Scene iv, beginning at the point
where Camillo questions Florizel and learns that he is
determined to 'put to sea' with Perdita (IV. iv. 509).
Then we have:

> *Flo.:*   Hark, Perdita (*drawing her aside*).[1]
> (*To Camillo*) I'll hear you by and by.
> *Cam.:*   He's irremoveable,
> Resolved for flight. Now were I happy, if
> His going I could frame to serve my turn.   (IV. iv. 517)

The conversation of Florizel and Perdita is required only
to cover Camillo's explanation of his motives and this
explanation is given to the audience in soliloquy, with
more than a tinge of direct address.[2] A little later the device
is repeated; Camillo has disclosed his plan and ends:

> For instance, sir,
> That you may know you shall not want, one word.
> (*They talk aside.*)
> (*Re-enter Autolycus.*)
> *Aut.:* Ha, ha! what a fool Honesty is!
> etc.   (IV. iv. 604)

At the end of his speech we have another stage direction:

[1] Stage directions are those of the editors, but they clearly represent the
'business' which Shakespeare intended. In the passages under discussion I
have added two extra directions taken from the *Shakespeare Head* edition to
those to be found in the *Globe* and *Arden* editions.

[2] 'Direct address' is the convention by which a character imparts information
in direct statement to the audience; *v. Shakespeare and the Popular Dramatic
Tradition*, Ch. V, pp. 84 *et seq.*

Camillo, Florizel, and Perdita come forward. There is no
natural occasion for this 'talk aside', since all three are
engaged in it; its only purpose is to allow Autolycus his
direct address to the audience on the gullibility of rustics.
Worst of all is the device to allow Camillo a last explanation
to the audience in an aside. Florizel exclaims:

> O Perdita, what have we twain forgot!
> Pray you, a word. (*They converse apart.*)   (IV. iv. 674)

We never hear what they have forgot, but Camillo steps
forward with

> What I do next, shall be to tell the king
> Of this escape . . .   (IV. iv. 676)

Florizel, Perdita and Camillo then go off, Autolycus has
more direct address to the audience and then we have his
meeting with Shepherd and Clown, in which the dialogue
is liberally bespattered with asides. In the end Autolycus
sends the others ahead of him to the seaside:

> Walk before toward the sea-side; go on the right hand: I will
> but look upon the hedge and follow you.   (IV. iv. 855)

Shepherd and Clown go, conversing in asides about
Autolycus, and Autolycus remains to tell the audience his
future plans.

I do not think anybody has tried to avoid the difficulty
raised here by calling in the usual hack assistant said to
have been responsible for Posthumus' dream in *Cymbeline*
and other such passages where it is supposed that Shakespeare has nodded – the dialogue is too clearly Shakespearean for that. Now it is hard to believe that Shakespeare
– even if tired, bored, cynical, in despair and dead drunk
at the time – could repeat a crudely amateur device like
this 'talking aside' or 'walking before' four times in a few
minutes and not intend something by it. Before the end
of the scene it has become laughable, and the laugh is
increased by the reason Autolycus gives for sending the
others ahead (i.e., the necessity of relieving himself); surely

D

this is a deliberately comic underlining of a deliberately crude technique. Considering now the play as a whole, are we not justified in suspecting a quite conscious return to naïve and outmoded technique, a deliberate creaking of the dramatic machinery? Are there not clear indications that it is an imitation naïveté after all?[1] *Exit, pursued by a bear!* How commentators have laughed at the slumbering Shakespeare, without noticing the comedy of Antigonus' vision, in which the eyes of the supposed dead Hermione 'became two spouts' (III. iii. 26)[2] in the manner of an earlier rhetoric, and without gauging the significance of the 'gentleman' on whom the bear had not yet half dined (III. iii. 108)! Perhaps we cannot claim as an old device the conventional impenetrability of disguise by reason of which Polixenes and Camillo move unrecognised among the shepherds; so useful a convention had long life on the stage. Autolycus, however, is an interesting dramatic throw-back. He is on terms of peculiar intimacy with the audience and so resembles the Vice of the interludes and Shakespeare's early clowns such as Launce and Lancelot Gobbo. At his first appearance he gives a summary history of himself:

> I have served Prince Florizel and in my time wore three-pile; but now I am out of service . . .
> My traffic is sheets; when the kite builds, look to lesser linen. My father named me Autolycus; who being, as I am, littered under Mercury, was likewise a snapper-up of unconsidered trifles. With die and drab I purchased this caparison, and my revenue is the silly cheat. Gallows and knock are too powerful on the highway: beating and hanging are terrors to me: for the life to come, I sleep out the thought of it.   (IV. iii. 13)

This is far away from even a modified naturalism; not only is it addressed directly to the audience but a person such as Autolycus would never in reality achieve such neat and

---

[1] Mr. Granville-Barker comes to a similar conclusion about the technique of *Cymbeline; v. Prefaces to Shakespeare, Second Series*, p. 243: 'it is obviously a sophisticated, not a native artlessness, the art that rather displays art than conceals it'.

[2] Dr. Tillyard is an honourable exception; *v. Shakespeare's Last Plays*, p. 77. So is Tinkler; *loc. cit.*, p. 362.

objective self-description. If, for instance, he 'sleeps out the thought' of the life to come, then he would hardly mention it; religious categories would not be in the forefront of his mind. From 'my traffic is in sheets' the speech, in effect, constitutes a 'character of a rogue' in the Theophrastan manner which had become popular, a description of a type in terms of seventeenth-century wit. It is in fact an admirable example of the blend of narrative and the representational, in which the character, as it were, tells his own story to the audience – a convention inherited from the medieval miracle plays.[1]

Why, then, did Shakespeare return so late in his career to this old-fashioned stage technique? I have already indicated internal evidence which suggests that the return was deliberate and this is confirmed by the fact that *The Winter's Tale* does not stand alone in respect of 'technical crudity'. Among a great many other instances we have 'Gower, as Chorus' in *Pericles* and Posthumus' dream in *Cymbeline*, both which Shakespeare permitted, whether he wrote them himself or not. *The Tempest* presents a different technique but with the same suggestion of inefficiency; we have a positive flaunting of the unities, yet coupled with the mildly comic tedium of Prospero's long narrative to the drowsily obedient Miranda. Even to preserve the unities Shakespeare need not have been so tedious – nor underlined the tedium by Miranda's apparent inattention, Prospero's protests and her assurances:

Pr.:   Thou attend'st not.
Mir.: O, good sir, I do.   (I. ii. 87)

Prospero the bore has left little for Prospero the magician to perform, for though he sends her magically to sleep he admits she is already 'inclined' to it (I. ii. 185). I imagine that Shakespeare's intention was to show that he could preserve the dramatic unities, about which there was so much critical cant, and at the same time mildly to bur-

[1] *V. Shakespeare and the Popular Dramatic Tradition*, Ch. IV, pp. 70 *et seq.*

lesque the extended narrative of past events which this
classical technique required.[1] What is more significant is
that he thus draws attention to the play as play by obtrud-
ing matters of technique upon the audience, and I believe
that in the previous romances the function of the old-
fashioned technique is precisely the same. If this should
seem unlikely, we may remember that as early as *Hamlet*
Shakespeare had used a burlesque of the older dramatists'
style to distinguish the 'Mousetrap' from the dialogue of
the main play. An audience in 1611 would react to some
aspects of *The Winter's Tale* (Antigonus' vision, his '*Exit,
pursued by a bear*' and the other examples I have mentioned) pretty much as a modern theatre audience reacts
to a burlesque revival of *Maria Martin* or *East Lynne*.

By deliberately drawing the audience's attention to
technique Shakespeare was able to distance his story and
to convey a continual reminder that his play was after all
only a play. The dialogue itself reinforces the duality of
play world and real world, as frequently in other plays of
Shakespeare; there is no need to believe this to have been
deliberate, though the reminders here seem specially
insistent. Time the Chorus is aware that his tale must seem
stale to 'the glistering of this present' (IV. i. 14), but this is
almost a reminder from without. Within the tale itself,
Mamillius would tell a story:

> A sad tale's best for winter: I have one
> Of sprites and goblins. (II. i. 25)

[1] Cf. Morton Luce's Introduction to *The Tempest* in the *Arden Shakespeare*,
pp. xxx-xxxi: 'As we have seen, *The Tempest* observes the unities of place and
time with a precision that must seem on the part of the author to be half
combative, half humorous. This we may gather from the many pointed references to the three or four hours' limit of the action, and it is possible that after
his most daring disregard of time and place in *The Winter's Tale* (which con-
tains, by the way, some equally pointed references to these particulars) the
poet wished – and again half defiantly, half humorously – to show how
exactly, if need were, his romantic plays could adjust themselves to the rigid
conventions of the classic drama. The classic prologue or chorus may also be
said to have their equivalent in *The Tempest*, as, for example, in the first part
of Act I, Scene ii.' It is interesting to note that this was written in 1901. The
whole introduction deserves study; it is an unusually perceptive piece of
critical writing.

There is a winter's tale within *The Winter's Tale*, recalling the play's title and reminding the audience that it is a play and not reality which confronts them.[1] The 'peripeteia' and 'discoveries' of the last act produce significant comment: 'this news which is called true is so like *an old tale* that the verity of it is in strong suspicion' (v. ii. 29), says the Second Gentleman. Later we have:

Second Gent.: What, pray you, became of Antigonus, that carried hence the child?

Third Gent.: Like *an old tale* still, which will have matter to rehearse, though credit be asleep and not an ear open. He was torn to pieces with a bear.

(v. ii. 64)

(For the soporific effect of an old tale we may compare Miranda as she suffers Prospero's long narrative.) The tone here is very delicate; there is an oblique apology for being tedious, and there is also a reminder – once again – of the play as play. Finally, in the last scene, where the 'coming to life' of the supposed statue of Hermione is markedly theatrical (it has further significance, however, in addition to its function as 'obvious' technique), Paulina says:

That she is living,
Were it but told you, should be hooted at
Like *an old tale:* but it appears she lives,
Though yet she speak not. (v. iii. 115)

Such internal comments upon the nature of a story always remind us of its unreality, breaking through any illusion which may have been created. Thus they combine with the deliberately old-fashioned technique to insist that it is after all only a dramatic performance that the audience have before them.

There are, I believe, a number of interlocking reasons for the unusually careful distancing of the play. I am not prepared to say how many of them may have been con-

[1] I have seen a film in which hero and heroine attend a cinema and see there a film of the same title as the main film. This would indicate that a modern popular audience is still open to the type of occult suggestion which such a situation mediates.

sciously in Shakespeare's mind as he wrote. He must have
been aware that he was using old-fashioned technique, but
it may be that all he intended was a pot-pourri entertainment including burlesque of the older drama. He seems
always to have written for the more intelligent members of
his audience and perhaps neither he nor they took the new
craze for romances very seriously; he may have set out to
produce a 'highbrow' comic version of the Beaumont and
Fletcher popular success – if Beaumont and Fletcher had
had enough successes at this time to have attracted his
notice. Perhaps he even deliberately designed that this
light entertainment should be at the same time profoundly serious, a poetic vehicle for philosophical and
religious truth. I want to make quite clear that all this is
highly speculative and is not my concern. A dramatist or
any other kind of artist may express meanings of which he
is himself only dimly aware and his methods may be dic-
tated by an end which he is not consciously seeking; the
real reason for his doing this or that can be discerned only
when the work is finished and understood. I do not know
what Shakespeare deliberately intended in this play; no
one can ever know and the question is not important.
What I am attempting to show is what in fact he did and
how he did it – the perhaps unconscious reasons which
led him to use one type of technique and reject another.

First, then, there is the nature of the story; 'an old tale'
may have its antiquity pressed home by the employment
of an outmoded technique. There are two ways of dealing
with historical material: one is to make it as realistic as
possible by presenting it in precisely the same way as one
would material from contemporary sources, and the other
is to emphasise its remoteness by adopting a certain
archaism in the means of presentation. Some historical
novelists, for example, write in a modern style, while others
prefer to suggest 'period' by an approximation to the
language of an earlier age – not necessarily the age they
are depicting. Shakespeare's is a double achievement: he

suggests antiquity by the methods I have just discussed, and suggests contemporaneity of interest through the verse. Secondly, this distancing indicates the sort of attention that the play demands. Shakespeare had always required close attention to the verse and the themes which it expressed; he had continually exploited the conventions of the theatre so as to reinforce in his audience an alert dual consciousness of play world and real world.[1] Nevertheless, with the tragedies it must have been difficult on first seeing them not to become wholly absorbed in character and action. Now, by exaggerated conventions and constant reminders of the play as play, he virtually forbids this sort of absorption; it is 'an old tale', remote from modern concerns; it is a play almost mockingly presented as a play, with the stage machinery innocently visible. We find it hard to become absorbed in characters which are dropped for a whole act at a time or which only appear half-way through the performance, and especially hard to become concerned over their fate when we may be called upon to laugh at an untimely end, as with the gentleman on whom the bear had not half dined. The course of events is too casually unfolded, with too many interruptions and asides, for a breathless anxiety such as we tend to feel over *Othello*. We are, in fact, quite firmly warned to seek our pleasure elsewhere; we are compelled to attend to the verse, to seek for 'inner meanings', to observe the subtle interplay of a whole world of interrelated ideas. Thirdly, as in the treatment of time, this is not only a means of commanding a special sort of attention but is also in itself a statement about the nature of reality.

Dr. Tillyard in *Shakespeare's Last Plays*[2] uses the phrase 'planes of reality' to describe the difference between the dream world of Leontes' jealousy, the religious world of the reported visit to the oracle and of the 'statue' scene,

---

[1] V. *Shakespeare and the Popular Dramatic Tradition*, *passim*, and especially Ch. II, pp. 31 *et seq.*

[2] Pp. 59 *et seq.*

the melodramatic vision of Antigonus and the earthy
comedy of the rustics. Before discussing this aspect of the
play I should like to point out the various planes of
reality revealed in relation to the contrast of play world
and real world – a matter which Dr. Tillyard comments
on all too briefly in dealing with *The Tempest* but omits
from his treatment of *The Winter's Tale*. This is a subject
which must have been constantly in Shakespeare's mind
and which receives its fullest and final statement in
Prospero's famous speech, 'Our revels now are ended',
after the performance of the Masque of Ceres (*The Tempest*,
IV. i. 148). 'On the actual stage,' says Dr. Tillyard, 'the
masque is executed by players pretending to be spirits,
pretending to be real actors, pretending to be supposed
goddesses and rustics.'[1] Prospero's speech then sees the
whole creation as a fading pageant (akin to the dream
world – another 'plane') and only the eternal remains as
the truly real.[2] In *The Winter's Tale*, if there is nothing to
equal Prospero's poetic statement, there is a sufficiently
complex presentation of the planes of reality. The audience
watch a dramatic performance of an old tale whose events
take place in the unreal world of romance yet are related
by literary means to their own real world. Within the play
itself characters speak of the old tale as being 'like an old
tale', which is both a reminder of the tale as just a tale
and also the opening up of a new degree of remoteness;
characters in an old tale speaking of an old tale carry a
suggestion of infinite regression. Again, there is Mamillius'
reference to 'a sad tale' which is 'best for winter' (II. i. 25)
and he even begins this tale within a tale: 'There was a
man. . . . Dwelt by a churchyard' (II. i. 29) – a man
suspiciously like the later Leontes.[3] Yet again we have
examples of Shakespeare's usual stage metaphor – the plane
of thought:

---

[1] *Ibid.*, p. 80.
[2] *V. Shakespeare and the Popular Dramatic Tradition*, Ch. II, pp. 40-41.
[3] Cf. Tinkler; *loc. cit.*, pp. 358, 361.

> Go, play, boy, play: thy mother plays, and I
> Play too, but so disgraced a part, whose issue
> Will hiss me to my grave.   (I. ii. 187)

> Methinks I play as I have seen them do
> In Whitsun pastorals: sure this robe of mine
> Does change my disposition.   (IV. iv. 133)

> . . . it shall be so my care
> To have you royally appointed as if
> The scene you play were mine.   (IV. iv. 602)

> I see the play so lies
> That I must bear a part.   (IV. iv. 669)

> No more such wives; therefore, no wife: one worse,
> And better used, would make her sainted spirit
> Again possess her corpse, and on this stage,
> Where we're offenders now, appear soul-vex'd,
> And begin, 'Why to me?'   (V. i. 56)

This last is the familiar Shakespearean identification of
this world with a stage, a metaphor carrying the suggestion
of a solider reality behind the visible world. Perdita's half-
bewildered remark:

> . . . sure this robe of mine
> Does change my disposition,

is interesting, especially in view of the Elizabethan convention by which disguise may alter the nature of the dis-
guised stage-personage – a convention of which a shadowy
trace may remain in Autolycus' complete change of personality with his change of garments, from pedlar-rogue
to upstart courtier, though this can in fact be explained
purely in terms of character criticism. We may further
note that Perdita for the sheep-shearing feast is acting
queen – a sort of May Queen – as for the 'Whitsun pas-
torals'; we have thus a characteristically Shakespearean
complication, for which the formula would be 'boy acting
girl who is a princess supposed to be a shepherdess acting
as make-believe princess'. The elaborate interconnection
of planes of reality here and throughout the play reveals
Shakespeare's interest in this further metaphysical problem

which is related to the problem of time. In *The Winter's
Tale* the two problems intersect and it is Time the Chorus
who completes the statement of relationship between the
various planes (though the statement is not really complete
until Prospero's great speech in *The Tempest*) by showing
the relativity even of that plane upon which the audience
find themselves; their fixed point disappears and they are
made to look back upon themselves from the remote future
as upon people in an old tale. It is necessary to be beyond
time in order to be beyond the possibility of illusion.

As we have said, Dr. Tillyard uses the same term,
'planes of reality', to cover shifts in the writer's presentation
of his subject. *The Winter's Tale* is remarkable for the
subtlety of these adjustments and they are best considered
now, since they are not unrelated to the planes of reality
I have just discussed and are sometimes mediated by the
seemingly crude dramatic technique which in this connection gains further significance. In the first brief scene
Camillo and Archidamus discuss the friendship of the two
kings and the 'unspeakable comfort' (i. i. 37) which the
country of Sicilia has in Mamillius, the young heir.
Mamillius, says Camillo, 'physics the subject, makes old
hearts fresh: they that went on crutches ere he was born
desire yet their life to see him a man'. The dialogue
continues:

> *Arch.:* Would they else be content to die?
> *Cam.:* Yes; if there were no other excuse why they should desire
>   to live.
> *Arch.:* If the king had no son, they would desire to live on crutches
>   till he had one.   (i. i. 46)

This is quite typical, a quietly humorous statement of the
ambiguity of human motives; the general devotion to
Mamillius is real enough but not more real than the
general devotion to a continued existence even upon
crutches. From the beginning seriousness is blent with
'wit' in the seventeenth-century sense – 'tough reasonable-
ness', as Mr. Eliot has described it in an essay on Marvell.

In the next scene jealousy descends suddenly upon
Leontes and he is isolated in a dream world of his own
projection; yet it is a dream which can be potent for evil
in the real world. Hermione in her clear-eyed virtue sums
up the position at her trial:

> My life stands in the level of your dreams,
> Which I'll lay down. (III. ii. 82)

Meanwhile Leontes within his dream regards himself as
aware of the real situation, though others similarly placed
may remain in ignorance:

> . . . many thousand on's
> Have the disease, and feel't not; (I. ii. 206)

and

> There may be in the cup
> A spider steep'd, and one may drink, depart,
> And yet partake no venom, for his knowledge
> Is not infected: but if one present
> The abhorr'd ingredient to his eye, make known
> How he hath drunk, he cracks his gorge, his sides,
> With violent hefts. I have drunk, and seen the spider.
> (II. i. 39)

Here is another problem concerning the nature of reality;
ignorance may be bliss and mistaken belief may carry all
the horrible consequences of objective ill. While Leontes
believes Hermione guilty, his belief brings about the same
consequences as if it were the truth; had she been guilty
and he not known it, their married life would not have
been jeopardised. Yet there *is* an objective truth – Shakespeare is no psychological relativist; Leontes is dreaming
and truth will out, for the divine oracle will declare it.

Paulina is an interesting character with something of a
'morality' flavour; she symbolises conscience, always at
Leontes' shoulder to prompt him to right conduct. Yet
she is a scold, presented as a comic figure, for the conscience
in its nagging persistence can be both comic and serious
at the same time. The third scene of Act II has some remark-

able variations in tone. It begins with the jealous Leontes
and in a vein of high seriousness:

> Nor night nor day no rest: it is but weakness
> To bear the matter thus . . .
>   . . . say that she were gone,
> Given to the fire, a moiety of my rest
> Might come to me again.   (II. iii. 1)

Paulina intrudes upon him against the will of Antigonus,
her husband. She brings with her the newly born girl-
child whom Leontes is determined to regard as bastard.
Leontes exclaims:

>   How!
> Away with that audacious lady! Antigonus,
> I charged thee that she should not come about me:
> I knew she would.   (II. iii. 41)

There is both comedy and pathos in the last four words.
Then follows a three-cornered dialogue upon Antigonus'
inability to rule his wife. The tone is lightened. Paulina
next breaks out into accusation of Leontes and presents
the child as his; he orders her to be put out of the room,
but apparently no one moves, for Leontes cries:

>   Traitors!
> Will you not push her out?   (II. iii. 72)

and turns on Antigonus, jeering at him as

>   . . . woman-tired, unroosted
> By thy dame Partlet here.   (II. iii. 74)

Paulina speaks again; then Leontes: 'He dreads his wife'
(II. iii. 79); then Paulina again; then Leontes: 'A nest of
traitors!' (II. iii. 81). Antigonus and Paulina both speak up
to repudiate the charge. Then Leontes exclaims against
Paulina:

>   A callat
> Of boundless tongue, who late hath beat her husband
> And now baits me!   (II. iii. 90)

The verse may be the verse of Leontes jealous but, in view
of what has gone before, the pun ('beat', 'bait') suggests a
further note of comedy. Yet he goes on to assert:

> This brat is none of mine;
> It is the issue of Polixenes:
> Hence with it, and together with the dam
> Commit them to the fire! (II. iii. 92)

His jealous fury by this bold juxtaposition is shown as itself essentially comic. Paulina vehemently maintains the legitimacy of the child, pointing out its resemblance to Leontes, but her speech ends with a joke, unconscious on Paulina's part but surely not on Shakespeare's: she prays that Nature may not reproduce in the infant her father's jealousy:

> . . . lest she suspect, as he does,
> Her children not her husband's. (II. iii. 107)

Malone comments solemnly on this passage: 'No suspicion that the babe in question might entertain of her future husband's fidelity could affect the legitimacy of her off-spring'.[1] He thinks that Shakespeare 'in the ardour of composition' has 'forgotten the difference of sexes' – which seems rather unlikely. It is, of course, the commentators who are at fault; their critical apriorism cannot accept the close interweaving of comedy and tragedy which is so important an element in the play. The slanging match continues, with more hard words about Antigonus' inability to control his wife:

> Leon.: A gross hag!
> And, lozel, thou art worthy to be hang'd,
> That wilt not stay her tongue.
> Ant.: Hang all the husbands
> That cannot do that feat, you'll leave yourself
> Hardly one subject. (II. iii. 108)

This is the perennial joke and the scene has reached something like a music-hall level of seriousness. Paulina has the last word and *exit*; Leontes turns to Antigonus again: 'Thou, traitor, hast set on thy wife to this . . .' (II. iii. 131). Antigonus speaks up, and the broil becomes general:

[1] V. *Variorum Shakespeare*, p. 106.

```
Ant.:                                    I did not, sir:
     These lords, my noble fellows, if they please,
     Can clear me in't.
Lords:                       We can: my royal liege,
     He is not guilty of her coming hither.
Leon.:  You're liars all.                      (II. iii. 141)
```

Leontes the tyrant has been shrewdly dealt with; as he says of Paulina:

```
                              Were I a tyrant,
     Where were her life?                      (II. iii. 122)
```

He recovers rapidly, however, and his disposal of the child is again quite serious in tone:

```
                    As by strange fortune
     It came to us, I do in justice charge thee,
     On thy soul's peril and thy body's torture,
     That thou commend it strangely to some place
     Where chance may nurse or end it. Take it up.
                                              (II. iii. 179)
```

This is firm, dignified and solemn, without the contorted jealousy rhythms and with no undercurrent of comedy. The scene ends, still quite seriously, with a report of the approach of Cleomenes and Dion newly returned from the oracle of Delphos.

The language associated with the oracle in the short scene which begins Act III introduces another plane of reality, the supernatural order, which also dominates the last scene of the play. Antigonus' vision suggests yet a further plane. It is distinguished from the play world around it by the employment of an old-fashioned rhetoric, so that the description of the vision suggests something theatrical and crude:

```
                    . . . she did approach
     My cabin where I lay; thrice bow'd before me,[1]
     And gasping to begin some speech, her eyes
     Became two spouts.                        (III. iii. 23)
```

---

[1] We are reminded of Pooh-bah and the unusually animated head, which
     . . . stood on its neck, with a smile well bred,
     And bow'd three times to me!

The ambiguity of the world of vision is stressed, for this is either a false vision (cf. Macbeth's 'fiend That lies like truth' (v. v. 43)) or else wrongly interpreted by Antigonus, who takes it to mean that 'Hermione hath suffer'd death' (III. iii. 42). Orthodox Christianity has always insisted on 'testing the spirits'; private visions must be tested by their congruency with divine revelation as interpreted by the Church. A vision might be (*a*) an objective presence, (*b*) subjective but sent from without, or (*c*) purely a projection and hallucinatory; if objective it might be angelic or diabolic or a soul out of purgatory, and if subjective but *ab extra* it might be sent by good or evil agency. In *Hamlet* and *Macbeth* Shakespeare had shown his interest in the subject, which was much debated in Elizabethan times.[1] Antigonus' vision is apropos in further complicating the planes of reality both through its comic tone and its theological ambiguity. No doubt the audience would incline to Antigonus' interpretation, except for the extreme protestants, who did not believe it possible for the dead to return to their former haunts, since they disbelieved in an 'intermediate state', and who were not the type to indulge in a 'willing suspension of disbelief' – but most probably they were not the type to attend the theatre at all. At the end of the play, however, if they carried their minds back to this ambiguous point, the audience would necessarily modify their opinion. The vision could then be regarded as angelic, since its directions for the disposal of Perdita were providentially effective, or as diabolic, since it led to the death of Antigonus and his company, Perdita alone escaping through her childhood innocence over which the devil could have no power. Not that an audience would reason so clearly upon the matter, but their reac-

[1] *V.* Professor Dover Wilson's discussion of Elizabethan theories about apparitions; *What Happens in Hamlet* (C.U.P., 1935), pp. 60 *et seq.*; also Walter Clyde Curry: *Shakespeare's Philosophical Patterns* (Louisiana State University Press, 1937), pp. 84 *et seq.*, where the same subject is dealt with in connection with the problem of Banquo's ghost. I am indebted to the scholarship of both these gentlemen in what I have written above.

tions would proceed against some such background of thought. The immediate dramatic purpose is, no doubt, to confirm the belief in Hermione's death and increase the effect of the *dénouement*, but the theological involvement adds to a general impression of the inadequacy of the human mind before the complex pattern of reality. We must not forget the note of burlesque; we are not to attach too much importance to the vision or to our speculations upon it – the great mystics are also sceptical about such visionary experiences.

Antigonus is summarily dismissed, 'pursued by a bear', and the most remarkable *volte-face* in the play – or perhaps in the whole of Shakespeare – now takes place. Certainly, as Dr. Tillyard says, the melodramatic vision has prepared the way by dissolving the reality of Antigonus, but it is none the less remarkable to find ourselves suddenly translated to the earthy comedy of the Bohemian rustics where Antigonus, whom we have followed with a degree of sympathy, becomes a gentleman on whom the bear has not half dined. The lost ship and its crew are similarly treated and the tempest, which Professor Wilson Knight has shown to be a constant symbol of tragedy in Shakespeare, suffers a comic transvaluation:[1]

> I would you did but see how it chafes, how it rages, how it takes up the shore! but that's not to the point. O, the most piteous cry of the poor souls! sometimes to see 'em, and not to see 'em; now the ship boring the moon with her main-mast, and anon swallowed with yest and froth, as you'ld thrust a cork into a hogshead. And then for the land-service, to see how the bear tore out his shoulder-bone; how he cried to me for help and said his name was Antigonus, a nobleman. But to make an end of the ship, to see how the sea flap-dragoned it: but, first, how the poor souls roared, and the sea mocked them; and how the poor gentleman roared and the bear mocked him, both roaring louder than the sea or weather.
>
> (III. iii. 89)

There is an interesting variety within this one speech.

[1] Tinkler speaks of the 'critical irony' in Shakespeare's treatment of the storm; *loc. cit.*, p. 362.

The tempest is at first tragic enough as it chafes and rages, the cry of the poor souls is piteous, the ship is carried to heaven, 'boring the moon with her main-mast'. Then comes a note of bathos; the tempest is compared to frothing liquor as a barrel is corked; it becomes familiar, friendly, and rather ridiculous; and from this point the sufferings of the sailors and of Antigonus are seen as trivial (the jesting 'land-service' marks the change); the sea and the bear become familiar monsters and the poor souls and the gentleman perish to the audience's laughter. This carries further the grotesque humour of Gloucester's attempted suicide in *King Lear*. There the apparent danger was purely imaginary – a parabolic suggestion that our human fears are needless, since we are in the hands of 'the clearest gods' (IV. vi. 73).[1] Here the same attitude is more directly presented. Subjectively, we are shown how much depends on point of view; how the tragic becomes comic, as later the comic becomes almost tragic in the old Shepherd's lament:

> You have undone a man of fourscore three,
> That thought to fill his grave in quiet . . . (IV. iv. 464)

Objectively, we are rendered suspicious of tragedy; *sub specie æternitatis* this being swallowed by the sea or by a bear may not be the dreadful matter we imagine it. Our silly pretensions distort the perspective; Antigonus, seized by a bear, cries out that he is a nobleman and the Clown refers to him punctiliously as 'the gentleman'. Gentlemen usually dine upon animals but now the bear will dine on the gentleman – an unusual version of 'Death the leveller'.

The general viewpoint of the scene is comic but there is a subtle mixture of attitudes, not only regarding the tragic tempest but regarding the comic rustics as well. Partly they are the stock stage types, a hitting-off of rustic simplicity, but there is a traditional rustic wisdom displayed by the Shepherd – Mr. Eliot's 'uncynical disillusion':

---

[1] *V.* G. Wilson Knight: *The Wheel of Fire* (O.U.P., *Second Impression*, 1937), pp. 187-188; and *Shakespeare and the Popular Dramatic Tradition*, p. 109.

E

I would there were no age between sixteen and three-and-twenty,
or that youth would sleep out the rest; for there is nothing in the
between but getting wenches with child, wronging the ancientry,
stealing, fighting . . .   (III. iii. 59)

And it is in the midst of such stuff as composes this scene
that Shakespeare is content to place a sentence central to
the significance of the whole play: 'Now bless thyself:
thou mettest with things dying, I with things new-born'
(III. iii. 116) – 'bless thyself', make the sign of the Cross,
for it is through the Cross that things dying are born again.

The sheep-shearing feast curiously blends the Florizel-
Perdita romance, the two generations of rustics, and
Autolycus. As Professor Dover Wilson has pointed out,
Florizel and Perdita are distinguished from the rustics
by their costume. Perdita has on her 'May Queen' robes and
Florizel's 'swain's wearing' is rich enough to transform
Autolycus later into a 'courtier cap-a-pe' (IV. iv. 761).[1]
Perhaps there is a hint here at the difference between
literary pastoral and genuine rusticity, as in the earlier
contrast between Silvius and Phebe and William and
Audrey. Although their romance has an element of tough
realism, as we shall see later, there is also a touch of comedy
in the dialogue itself which is perhaps critical of the false
high seriousness of fashionable Arcadia. In *Pandosto*
Greene's Prince Dorastus has a speech on the metamorphoses of the gods: 'The heavenly gods have sometime
earthly thoughts. Neptune became a ram, Jupiter a bull,
Apollo a shepherd: they gods and yet in love . . .'[2] It
has often been noted that Shakespeare borrows the speech
but no one has commented on the significant changes in
Florizel's version:

Jupiter
Became a bull, and bellow'd; the green Neptune
A ram, and bleated . . .   (IV. iv. 27)

---

[1] V. *New Cambridge Shakespeare*, p. 165. The explanation of Florizel's 'swain's
wearing' was communicated to Professor Wilson by Mr. Granville-Barker.

[2] V. *Greene's 'Pandosto' or 'Dorastus and Fawnia'*, ed. P. G. Thomas (Chatto
and Windus, 1907), p. 56; or *Variorum Shakespeare*, pp. 343 *et seq*. (The latter
version retains the original spelling.)

'Bellow'd' and 'bleated' have a comic and satiric force reflecting unfavourably upon the pagan deities which were treated so seriously in contemporary pastoral.

The sheep-shearing feast is followed immediately by theatrical plans for escape and Autolycus' satire on the court. In the fifth act the first scene sustains the serio-comic tension in Paulina and the second scene recounts at second hand in a burlesque version of court jargon the all-important discovery of Perdita's true identity, her restoration to Leontes and the meeting of the two kings in reconciliation. This not only saves the climax for the last scene but in itself adds another plane of reality: 'news', 'gossip', inevitably distorted in transmission. The last scene, theatrically posed, has the religious tone associated previously with the oracle; now it is carried to new heights in the reunion of Leontes and Hermione.

Before passing on to the interpretation of the play, I should like to re-emphasise one fact: all that has been considered so far as to the treatment of time, stagecraft and 'planes of reality' has revealed not only a method of dramatic presentation but also a statement, complex and profound, of the nature of reality. This fusion of method and statement is the last degree of organic unity. The significances in verse and story which I am to consider in Part II must be taken with these statements about time and reality if the play's full content is to be appreciated.

PART TWO

Interpretation

TO INTERPRET a play of Shakespeare it is necessary to examine the course of the story in close relation to the verse in which it is expressed, for the story gains significance through the implications of the verse. This method is not fool-proof and there is no possibility of 'scientific' objectivity; devotion to the text, however, acts as some check upon individual imagination. There may be danger of 'reading in' more than the verse can bear, but this tendency can be restrained by an acquaintance with Elizabethan thought and language. Inevitably we must penetrate below the writer's conscious intention, for, as I have said before, poets frequently mean more than they are aware of meaning; the best safeguards here are common sense and a critical attitude towards the Freudian. An interpretation which follows this method is, I believe, likely to be nearer the truth than one based only upon the broad outline of a play, for an outline may look very different when the detail has been properly considered.

My friend and former colleague, Professor D. G. James, in *Scepticism and Poetry*,[1] an important essay on the poetic imagination, devotes an interesting and valuable chapter to Shakespeare's last plays. Mr. James believes that in the romances Shakespeare is trying to express the meaning of life in a 'mythology' of his own. 'Mythology' he defines as 'a mode of saying something which evades lucid and intelligible expression in the prose of statement'[2] and he suggests that Shakespeare, having something of this sort to say and unwilling to make use of traditional Christian dogma, sought symbolic expression in the romantic tales from *Pericles* to *The Tempest*. The general similarity of these tales

[1] George Allen and Unwin, 1937.
[2] *Op. cit.*, p. 213.

indicates either a failure of Shakespeare's invention or that
he wished to insist on certain elements that they have in
common and which best expressed his view of human life.
Mr. James prefers the latter hypothesis and isolates certain
symbolic themes. The fundamental theme is the finding of
what is lost (Perdita in *The Winter's Tale*), which signifies
the loss of the soul through evil and its final restoration.
Related to this is the theme of royalty; royalty is lost and
restored, a royal personage is lost and then sought out and
restored by another royal personage (Perdita and Florizel).
The preservation of helpless infants (Perdita again, in *The
Winter's Tale*) suggests the resolution of human tragedy,
and the return of the dead to life is another constantly
repeated symbol; Mr. James does not make its significance
quite clear but I think he believes it to refer to the life
after death.

There is certainly significance in Shakespeare's repeated
use of romantic tales in this last period of his active life –
I have already considered their appropriateness to his
general purpose – and there is probably more than general
significance in their possessing in common the themes
isolated by Mr. James. But I think there is a certain danger
in abstracting the symbolic themes from their poetic
embodiment and pointing to them as Shakespeare's
'meaning' in these plays. Mr. James, indeed, is modest
and apologetic as he does so, since he believes himself to
be endeavouring to state abstractly something which by
his own definition 'evades lucid and intelligible expression
in the prose of statement'. My own objection would not
be based on the impossibility of translating a 'mythology'
into abstract terms or expressing 'in the prose of statement'
an abstract of poetic experience; these processes are quite
valid provided the result is realised to be only an intellectual signpost – not in any sense equivalent to the original
but a general indication of what may be found in it.
Shakespeare's verse, however, is so crammed with meaning
that the significance that the story in outline seems to bear

may be materially different from its significance in the full poetic context of the play. Mr. James produces an almost allegorical interpretation of the last plays by considering the symbolic meaning of the personages and main events largely apart from the poetry in which they are presented. His treatment of the theme of royalty exemplifies what seems to me to be the inadequacy of the method. In *Pericles* 'we are aware of the high destiny of the soul in and through the symbol of royalty';[1] 'royalty is a symbol for what is spiritual'.[2] But in *The Winter's Tale* (and *The Tempest*) the love theme confuses the use of this symbol, since the lover-prince is prepared to sacrifice royalty for love. 'The symbol therefore has two significances; the first as a signification of the divine destiny of the soul, and secondly, of all worldly values which the royalty of the pure spirit discounts'.[3] There is confusion in the symbolism, says Mr. James, and this arises from the inadequacy of the symbol of royalty to its original function. It is, we note, in *Pericles*, an inferior play, that the symbolic expression is said to be clearest, whereas in *The Winter's Tale* it is relatively confused. It may be, then, that clarity of symbolism is less important than Mr. James would have us believe.

I suppose that the integrity of the royalty symbol in *The Winter's Tale* might be maintained by pointing out that he who would save his life must lose it, that it is the willingness to lose royalty which is instrumental in saving it. This would be one way of regarding Florizel's flight with Perdita; but I cannot believe that Shakespeare intended to burden himself with anything even approaching the allegorical. Had he employed symbols bearing one clear and consistent intellectual meaning throughout the play, he would necessarily have limited the range and subtlety of his poetry. Allegorical verse with its stress on intellectual correspondence tends towards a conscious formality which has virtues of its own but certainly not the

<hr>

[1], [2], [3] *Ibid.*, p. 223.

characteristically Shakespearean virtues. Nevertheless, I feel
sure that these themes had special significance for Shakespeare. The finding of what is lost is never in point of fact
a human finding but a divine disclosure – Perdita is found
by Leontes, not Florizel; Florizel woos but does not 'seek'
her, and her restoration is in fulfilment of the oracle after
the pious submission of Hermione. The protection of the
innocent is again a strong manifestation of overruling
providence. Royalty to Shakespeare's ardently royalist
mind may have been associated with the *donum super-
additum* by which, according to scholastic theology, a
human soul is made capable of the vision of God. This is
very doubtful, however, for Leontes loses his daughter,
or rather causes her to be lost, but does not lose his royal
prerogative, only his hope of an heir. The return of the
supposed dead to life certainly suggests the doctrine of the
resurrection; no doubt Shakespeare is thinking of life after
death, but there may also be a hint of the Pauline doctrine
in which the Christian life on earth is a resurrected life,
baptism implying the death of the 'old man' and a new
birth in Christ. It seems more than likely that associations
of this kind would influence Shakespeare in choosing these
romantic tales as vehicles for his maturest reflection about
life, and I hope to confirm this hypothesis later. But,
whereas Mr. James treats such symbolism on the conceptual plane as almost allegorical in function, I should prefer
to regard it as hinted in the poetry but never self-consciously worked out, not regulative of the play's meaning
though contributing towards it. All poetry tends to be
symbolic; there are different degrees of self-consciousness
in the poetic use of symbols, from the mere description
that has yet a touch of something more – the English
countryside in *L'Allegro*, which is at the same time a land
of heart's desire – to the complete allegorical panoply of
the *Divina Commedia* or the *Roman de la Rose*. Even in the
last plays Shakespeare's use of symbols is very much less
rational and self-conscious than Dante's, and it is because

he is not tied to a conceptual scheme that the same symbol
– that of royalty, for instance – may combine different
significances without contradiction. His symbols are the
richer for being less explicit (richer than almost all allegory, though I should hesitate over the multifold meanings
of Dante) and what Mr. James calls confusion might well
be commended as a happy fertility of poetic imagination.

It is, I think, because of his method of interpretation
that Mr. James is led to certain adverse judgments on the
last plays in addition to the complaint about confused
symbolism: 'What Shakespeare was anxious to convey he
attempted to convey at the expense of his art, about which
he seems in these plays to have cared little'.[1] We are told,
for instance, that 'Paulina's deception of Leontes and
imprisonment of Hermione is preposterous'.[2] Of course,
Hermione was not imprisoned by Paulina but went into
voluntary retirement, and, if the whole long incident is
far-fetched, it is quite consistent with the carefully built up
atmosphere of the 'old tale'. 'And the coming to life of the
"dead",' we are told, 'obsessed his imagination to the
point of making his work silly to a degree it never had
before been.'[3] On the contrary, the theatricality of the
'statue' scene in *The Winter's Tale* (to take the example
which immediately concerns us) implies a delicate admission of inadequacy which is itself part of the meaning of the
play; only in an artificial, deliberately formalised scene
could such religious significance be conveyed without
spiritual indelicacy. The hushed and awesome verse in its
simplicity and strength supports the ritual suggestion of the
setting.

My last objection to Mr. James relates to the wider
question of Shakespeare's 'mythology'. I cannot see any
advantage in confusing the mythopœic power of a primi-
tive community with the imagination of a civilised poet

[1] *Ibid.*, p. 233.
[2] *Ibid.*, pp. 232-233.
[3] *Ibid.*, p. 233.

and I should prefer not to use the term 'mythology' in connection with Shakespeare at all. But this is a minor matter. Conceding the term, I remain unhappy with the substance of Mr. James' thought on the subject. 'Shakespeare,' he says, 'having failed to see human life as a neat, orderly, and satisfying unity, had resort to myth for the conveyance of his new imaginative apprehension of life. But his mythology was not Christian; as long as he wrote poetry he tried to maintain its independence of traditional forms.'[1] If this means only that Shakespeare never thought of writing a miracle play but kept to the form of the secular drama, then, of course, it is unexceptionable. Or, again, Mr. James may mean that Shakespeare avoided in his last plays a too deliberate use of traditional Christian symbolism, as Mr. T. S. Eliot has done in the poems from *Burnt Norton* to *Little Gidding*. But if he means, rather, that Shakespeare aimed at providing a mythology interpretative of human experience as an alternative to the Christian dogmatic scheme, I should be compelled to disagree. We have already seen that Shakespeare does not wholly avoid explicit reference to Christian dogma in *The Winter's Tale* and I hope, by examining the poetic development of the story, to show that it does in fact follow the Christian scheme of redemption. It is not a new mythology that the play presents – not a new interpretation of human experience but the old interpretation newly translated into terms of the romance and all the more faithfully for its synthesis of pagan beauty and Christian truth.

II – SIN AND REPENTANCE

THE PLAY begins with Leontes and Polixenes renewing their childhood friendship; we hear in the first scene of Mamillius, the young heir of Sicilia, beloved of the people, and the

[1] *Ibid.*, p. 210.

next scene opens with Leontes and his queen urging
Polixenes to stay 'one seven-night longer' (I. ii. 17). For a
short time there is an atmosphere of pleasant sophistica-
tion with Hermione engaged in light-hearted repartee.
Polixenes' reference to his early friendship with Leontes –
'We were as twinn'd lambs that did frisk i' the sun'
(I. ii. 67) – employs the traditional symbol of innocence
(*Agnus Dei, qui tollis peccata mundi*) linked closely with a
reference to original sin:

> . . . we knew not
> The doctrine of ill-doing, nor dream'd
> That any did. Had we pursued that life,
> And our weak spirits ne'er been higher rear'd
> With stronger blood, we should have answer'd heaven
> Boldly 'not guilty'; the imposition clear'd
> Hereditary ours.   (I. ii. 69)

Then follow the references to grace already noticed in the
treatment of so-called anachronism.[1] I do not suggest that
these images and references are to be wrested into a plain
theological meaning but merely that by these means the
audience are prepared (unconsciously for the most part)
to seek religious significance in what follows. Before
Leontes falls into jealousy the notions of original and
actual sin, innocence, guilt and divine grace have all been
touched on, without any direct theological statement and
mainly in jest. This is typical of Shakespeare's oblique
expression, as Dr. Tillyard might call it,[2] in *The Winter's
Tale*.

Hermione succeeds in persuading Polixenes to stay.
'At my request he would not,' says Leontes (I. ii. 87),
and, although the jealousy has not yet come upon him and
all is outwardly gay, a change is poetically prepared, as
Tinkler shows,[3] in the rather unpleasant flavour of the
imagery:

---

[1] *V*. Part I, pp. 38-39, *supra*.
[2] *V. Poetry Direct and Oblique* (Chatto and Windus, 1934), *passim*.
[3] *Loc. cit.*, p. 359.

> . . . cram's with praise, and make's
> As fat as tame things;   (I. ii. 91)

> Three crabbed months had sour'd themselves to death.
>   (I. ii. 102)

Then suddenly with no more hint of preparation[1] – and no hint at all on the psychological plane – Leontes' jealousy comes full upon him:

> Too hot, too hot!
> To mingle friendship far is mingling bloods.
> I have tremor cordis on me . . .   (I. ii. 108)

This is his sin, the sin of sexual jealousy, and it comes upon him with no warning, apparently from without. The lack of motivation cannot be ascribed to the exigencies of the Elizabethan drama; an address to the audience could have summarised Leontes' psychological history, like Gloucester's opening soliloquy in *Richard III*. But Shakespeare seems never to have been content with mere psychology. Sin comes from without, as in the Christian scheme it comes from the temptation of the devil – we are concerned, I think, with the general origin of evil as well as with the origin of this particular sin in Leontes. Leontes' sin comes unmotivated, but sin is necessarily without any truly rational foundation.[2] *Quidquid petitur, petitur sub specie boni:* if, therefore, evil is chosen, evil has been seen as a good; everything has been seen in false perspective, so that such a choice must be unmotivated in the sense that it is devoid of adequate motive. Moreover, sinful thoughts such as this unwarranted sexual jealousy, though they may not in reality spring fully grown into the mind, may well emerge with baffling suddenness into the consciousness. We are thus shown

---

[1] *V.* Appendix A.

[2] Cf. St. Thomas Aquinas: *Summa Theologica*, Prima Secundæ, Quæst. LXXXVI, Art. I: 'Cum autem peccat, adhæret aliquibus rebus contra lumen rationis, et divinæ legis . . .'

Leontes' jealousy (a) metaphysically, as it appears *sub specie æternitatis*, and (b) as it appears to Leontes himself and presumably to those about him. We are not shown its psychological growth, since its psychological origins are not in question. In this Shakespeare is more natural than the naturalists. The naturalistic playwright, pledged to psychological determinism, attempts to show the growth of the passions on the stage and is too frequently reduced to an obviousness and lack of restraint which travesties civilised behaviour. Shakespeare does not reveal those secret mental processes, unknown to others and un-suspected by the victim himself, by which a sinful judg-ment slowly germinates in the mind; towards such spiritual mysteries he preserves an attitude of reverent agnosticism. Hamlet's resentment at those who would 'pluck out the heart of his mystery' (III. ii. 382) may reflect his creator's sense of the inviolable depths of human personality. Shakespeare explores the countries of the mind as an artist – perhaps a more profitable activity than the psycho-logical ordnance survey.

The jealousy once asserted, we are given a close meta-physical study of it, reaching depths undreamed of in the days of *Othello*. In *Othello* the verse disintegrated under the strain of jealous passion into broken, inarticulate prose; the verse here writhes and bends but remains a tense, taut medium of objective expression, leading us to expect analysis rather than direct representation of Leontes' mental state. The imagery suggests nerves which quiver unheathily; beginning in imagination directed towards the supposed lovers ('paddling palms and pinching fingers' (I. ii. 115)), this hypersensitivity goes on to record the irritant effect of jealous thoughts which are to Leontes 'goads, thorns, nettles, tails of wasps' (I. ii. 329).[1] We hear later of sleeplessness – 'Nor night nor day no rest' (II. iii. 1) – which, the physical result of a mental unease, is in Shakespeare the usual accompaniment of sin. Macbeth in

[1] Cf. Tinkler; *loc. cit.*, p. 354.

murdering Duncan 'murdered sleep' (II. ii. 36) and, as
later he sought relief from insomnia in the liquidation of
doubtful adherents, so Leontes says that once Hermione
is burnt

> a moiety of my rest
> Might come to me again.   (II. iii. 8)

As he dwells on the theme of adultery his expression has
the violence and crudity of disgust:

> No barricado for a belly; know't;
> It will let in and out the enemy
> With bag and baggage: many thousand on's
> Have the disease, and feel't not;   (I. ii. 204)

> . . . say
> My wife's a hobby-horse, deserves a name
> As rank as any flax-wench that puts to
> Before her troth-plight.   (I. ii. 275)

Writers of the 'twenties, fired with the duty of 'debunking',
and substituting psycho-analysis for literary criticism,
found in Leontes proof of the elderly Shakespeare's 'sex-
disgust'. This was a grave charge, sex-disgust being the
only mortal sin which the 'twenties recognised. Not un-
naturally, however, it is a sin into which very few outside
the 'twenties seem to have fallen. The disgust is clearly
Leontes', not Shakespeare's; the healthy sensuality of
Perdita is as obviously approved as the Leontes disgust is
discredited. And even Leontes' disgust is not directed at
sexuality but at sexual sin – it is not his moral attitude
which is wrong; it is his obsession with sexual sin, resulting
from his wrong judgment upon Hermione. But with our
immediate elders, an you speak ill of adultery, how they
take it at heart! The theme of disease is persistent during
Leontes' jealousy, but not sexual disease as in *Troilus and
Cressida*. The disease image is used in three several con-
nections: to be a cuckold is to 'have the disease' (I. ii. 207);
so is to be an adulteress:

> . . . were my wife's liver
> Infected as her life, she would not live
> The running of one glass;[1]   (I. ii. 304)

and, more important, Leontes himself according to Camillo
is diseased in 'opinion' (I. ii. 297). The most fatal consequence of Leontes' evil opinion is his separation from the
rest of the world; he becomes estranged not only from
Hermione and Polixenes but from his children and from
the whole court. I examined earlier the half comic rebellion
of Paulina and the courtiers against their 'tyrant', who
cuts a miserable figure isolated in the dream world of his
own distorted judgment. Sin separates the sinner from God
and what is God-like; at the same time, like every category
of evil, not being of God it has no existence but is a nega-
tion or perversion of existence; such is the orthodox
Christian opinion as most exactly expressed in St. Thomas
Aquinas.[2] Leontes' sin is that he mistakes Hermione's
graciousness for unlawful love. So long as he harbours this
belief it governs his experience and distorts his vision;
his sense of order and proportion is gone,[3] so that his
universe is no longer the common universe in which the
others live but a dream world which he and he alone takes
for reality:

> How blest am I
> In my just censure, in my true opinion!   (II. i. 36)

he says. But to Hermione he is dreaming, though his dream
impinges dangerously upon the actual world: 'My life
stands in the level of your dreams' (III. ii. 82). Leontes
replies with 'Your actions are my dreams' (III. ii. 83) – the
perfect inversion of reality. Paulina with her reputation

---

[1] It is interesting to note in so serious a context the traditional 'life, liver'
pun which remains a familiar chestnut.

[2] V. Summa Theologica, Pars Prima, Quæst. XLVIII, Art. I, Conclusio:
'Non existens aliquid, vel natura aliqua, sed ipsa boni absentia malum est'.
And v. Note 3, inf.

[3] Cf. Summa Theologica, Prima Secundæ, Quæst. LXXV, Art. I: 'peccatum
est quidam actus inordinatus'.

F

for plain speaking calls him 'mad' (II. iii. 71), refers to his 'weak-hinged fancy' (II. iii. 119) and later to his

> Fancies too weak for boys, too green and idle
> For girls of nine.   (III. ii. 182)

To be diseased in judgment so as to take good for ill (a more serious matter ultimately than the committing of known sin) is to have cast loose from reality; the real gravity of moral failure lies in its metaphysical implications. Practical ill consequences involving others must also follow from inhabiting a distorted world; Leontes piles up his score of sin[1] in ordering the murder of Polixenes, in seeking the death of Hermione and in the exposure of his child; and the effects of his bad dream are felt by his wife and children, by Camillo, who is exiled, by Antigonus and his wife, Paulina, and by the whole nation, since their king is now without an heir.

Because his opinion is not based firmly upon reality, Leontes, though strenuously assertive in the face of incredulity, is yet 'a feather for each wind that blows' (II. iii. 154). His sending to the oracle 'for a greater confirmation' (II. i. 180) is perhaps not entirely, as he says, to 'give rest to the minds of others' (II. i. 191). Hermione's clear vision, firmness and patience contrast strongly with the ill-judged precipitancy of her husband:

> How will this grieve you,
> When you shall come to clearer knowledge, that
> You thus have publish'd me! Gentle my lord,
> You scarce can right me throughly then to say
> You did mistake.   (II. 1. 96)

Here are the Christian virtues. She goes to prison 'for her better grace' (II. i. 122) and the court, as she goes, spontaneously protest her innocence.

The short scene beginning Act III marks a turning point in the play. The oracle of Apollo is poetically built up into

---

[1] Cf. *Summa Theologica*, Prima Secundæ, Quæst. LXXXV, Art. III: 'Ex hoc enim quod anima deordinatur per peccatum præcedens, facilius inclinatur ad peccandum'.

a symbol of God's overruling providence, and for the first
time we see the Leontes situation from the outside and
realise that it is under control. Tinkler has noted[1] the
resemblance between the poetry here and at the entry of
Duncan into Macbeth's castle (a passage whose religious
symbolism has been excellently treated by Dr. F. R.
Leavis[2]). Here the scene begins:

> The climate's delicate, the air most sweet,
> Fertile the isle . . .   (III. i. 1)

The rhythm is quietly detached. Good climate, sweet air
and fertility suggest metaphysical goodness and the divine
creative power; they must always have been associated
with some form of divine beneficence in pagan times, and
in Holy Scripture abundant crops frequently symbolise
the activity of God, as in the parable of the Sower. Shakespeare seems to have followed traditional usage, since in
Macbeth to the venerable Duncan:

>   . . . the air
> Nimbly and sweetly recommends itself,   (I. vi. 1)

and from Banquo we hear that

>   This guest of summer,
> The temple-haunting martlet, does approve,
> By his loved mansionry, that the heaven's breath
> Smells wooingly here: no jutty, frieze,
> Buttress, nor coign of vantage, but this bird
> Hath made his pendent bed and procreant cradle:
> Where they most breed and haunt, I have observed,
> The air is delicate.   (I. vi. 3)

The significant words are: 'Nimbly and sweetly', 'temple-
haunting', 'wooingly', 'bed and procreant cradle', 'breed',
'delicate'. In *The Winter's Tale* we have 'delicate', 'sweet',
'fertile', carrying the same suggestion, and the subsequent
lines express more of the quality of religious feeling than

---

[1] *Loc. cit.*, pp. 351-352.
[2] *How to Teach Reading* (Minority Press, 1932), pp. 29 *et seq.*

the *Macbeth* passage, adding supernatural awe to the
recognition of immanent divinity:

>   I shall report,
> For most it caught me, the celestial habits,
> Methinks I so should term them, and the reverence
> Of the grave wearers. O, the sacrifice!
> How ceremonious, solemn and unearthly
> It was i' the offering.   (III. i. 3)

We have here a number of epithets evocative of religious
awe: 'celestial', 'grave' and especially 'ceremonious,
solemn and unearthly'. The whole speech with its reference
to priestly garments and the offering of a sacrifice, together
with the epithets just quoted, sounds almost like a description of the Mass.[1] Power is expressed in

> . . . the ear-deafening voice o' the oracle,
> Kin to Jove's thunder,   (III. i. 9)

which, Cleomenes says,

>   so surprised my sense,
> That I was nothing –   (III. i. 10)

the familiar mystical annihilation of self in the presence of
God. The rest of the scene, in which the oracle is discussed
in relation to Hermione, further establishes this religious
awe ('rare, pleasant, speedy . . . Great Apollo Turn all
to the best! . . . Apollo's great divine . . . gracious be
the issue!'). Dion's last words – 'And gracious be the

---

[1] 'Habits' seems to be Dion's (or Shakespeare's) attempt at technical
language. His hesitancy – 'Methinks I so should term them' – is justified;
'vestments' would be more correct. If Shakespeare had an elaborately ceremonious mass in mind, he must have experienced it abroad or relied on
travellers' descriptions, unless he was thinking of the Anglican rite as performed in the Chapel Royal and the private chapel of Bishop Andrewes.
Before Archbishop Laud the usual celebration of the Anglican rite would
hardly fit Dion's description. The secret masses of recusant Roman Catholics
cannot have been elaborate in ceremonial, though mass vestments would be
worn and the normal ceremonies prescribed for the priest would certainly be
carried out. To a recusant such a service would be a rare privilege, and the
more impressive for the contrasting atmosphere of suspicion and danger
surrounding it. It is not impossible that Shakespeare, even if himself an Anglican,
had a secret celebration of the Mass in his memory as he wrote Dion's speech.
If Smart is right about John Shakespeare's recusancy, the young William may
have attended Mass with his father in such conditions.

issue!' (III. i. 22) – remind us of the repeated references to
grace in previous scenes; at the end of this present scene
grace can be taken only in its full theological sense, as a
power for good infused by God into the soul.

At her trial Hermione remains patient and dignified
towards men, humble and strong in faith towards God –
a pattern of Christian sanctity:

> . . . if powers divine
> Behold our human actions, as they do,
> I doubt not then but innocence shall make
> False accusation blush and tyranny
> Tremble at patience.   (III. ii. 29)

In the second line the last three words are strongly
accented and being monosyllabic demand slow enuncia-
tion; in the first folio they were printed in brackets for
emphasis.[1] It is a strong assertion of religious faith.
She is unafraid, but anxious to clear her name:

> . . . no life,
> I prize it not a straw, but for mine honour,
> Which I would free . . .   (III. ii. 110)

Her whole trust is in the oracle of Apollo:

> Your honours all,
> I do refer me to the oracle:
> Apollo be my judge!   (III. ii. 115)

As certain officers depart to bring in the oracle, during
the moment of tension, she thinks of her father:

> The Emperor of Russia was my father:
> O that he were alive, and here beholding
> His daughter's trial! that he did but see
> The flatness of my misery, yet with eyes
> Of pity, not revenge!   (III. ii. 120)

This is not addressed to any one in particular and it is
perhaps unlikely that an Hermione would reveal such
intimate feeling in public. Here, as in many other places
in Shakespeare, we have to do with a convention not
unlike the recent dramatic experiment of 'expressionism'.

---

[1] V. *New Cambridge Shakespeare*, p. 151.

Hermione speaks out for the audience's sake what is in her mind, though in reality she would probably have kept silence. Shakespeare at such times differs from the modern expressionist only in being less consciously aware of his method and so capable of reverting to normal dialogue without the abrupt transitions noticeable in Eugene O'Neill's *Strange Interlude*. With all her courage, her patience and her faith Hermione is in 'flat misery', yet even at such a time it is 'pity' she desires, 'not revenge'.

The oracle is read:

> Hermione is chaste; Polixenes blameless; Camillo a true subject; Leontes a jealous tyrant; his innocent babe truly begotten; and the king shall live without an heir, if that which is lost be not found.
>
> (III. ii. 133)

It is sufficiently oracular, but the ways of Providence are dark. We may be impressed again by the crudity of this pagan machinery and its inadequacy for the expression of Christian thought. But the very crudity is a reminder of the inadequacy of the human intellect and the necessity of submission to the divine will. I suppose Shakespeare could have dared on the stage what Milton dared in *Paradise Lost*; in a way there was 'example for't' in the miracle cycles. But, instead of striving to surpass the necessary limitations of his art, he accepts them fully, incorporating them as a part of his theme; such at least seems to be implied in the pagan oracle. To object to Shakespeare's inadequate means is to miss the fine humility of his mature mind, beside which the sublimity of Milton, justifying the ways of God, seems even less adequate because not sufficiently aware of its own inadequacy:

> . . . here on this lowly ground,
> Teach mee how to repent . . .[1]

Leontes now adds to his sin a blasphemous disbelief in revelation: 'There is no truth at all i' the oracle' (III. ii. 141). At once he is punished with the death of Mamillius and the apparent death of Hermione. Hermione's sixteen years'

---

[1] In the seventh of Donne's *Holy Sonnets*.

separation from her beloved husband is in obedience to
the oracle, for the king must live without an heir unless
Perdita should be restored to him. It is a voluntary sacrifice, but the divine gifts to humanity are in part contingent
upon such self-abnegation in the saints. As for Mamillius,
we are reminded that every sin must have its inevitable
consequence. The young prince resembled his father
closely:

> . . . they say we are
> Almost as like as eggs;   (I. ii. 129)

it is as if something of Leontes has died before the half-life
of his sixteen years' penance. Again, we are made to see
how widespread the effect of sin may be, since the death
of Mamillius leaves Leontes without an heir and this is an
unsatisfactory state of affairs for the whole land; in Act v
Leontes still thinks of the sin

> . . . which was so much,
> That heirless it hath made my kingdom.   (v. i. 9)

To a believer in the *jus divinum* the king may be identified
with his country; when the king suffers, so does the country,
and *vice versa*. Moreover, Shakespeare had lived through
the later years of Queen Elizabeth and knew the dangers
of an uncertain succession. Perhaps he wrote so much of
kings not merely in obedience to the Aristotelian require-
ment of nobility in a tragic hero but because he could best
communicate through such characters the truth that our
actions, whether good or ill, have remoter consequences
bearing upon the whole society to which we belong. Thus
Scotland under Macbeth is apostrophised:

> O nation miserable,
> With an untitled tyrant bloody-scepter'd,
> When shalt thou see thy wholesome days again . . . ?
>   (IV. iii. 103)

while of Edward the Confessor it is said that

> . . . sundry blessings hang about his throne,
> That speak him full of grace.   (IV. iii. 158)

So in *The Winter's Tale* we are concerned with the fall and restoration of Leontes and of his kingdom; Polixenes speaks of

> that fatal country, Sicilia . . . whose very naming punishes me with the remembrance of that penitent, as thou callest him, and reconciled king, my brother; whose loss of his most precious queen and children are even now to be afresh lamented.   (IV. ii. 22)

There is no need to go very far with Tinkler in applying the Waste Land legend to Leontes' story; the sacramental idea of monarchy, familiar enough to the England of James I, supplies all that we need in this connection. Indeed, we have a direct reminder of the doctrine in Camillo's refusal to poison Polixenes:

> —If I could find example
> Of thousands that had struck anointed kings
> And flourish'd after, I'ld not do't; but since
> Nor brass nor stone nor parchment bears not one,
> Let villany itself forswear't.   (I. ii. 357)

Leontes' repentance is as sudden as his first jealousy, though clearly motivated by the severe judgment which has fallen upon him. He begins anew, in verse smoothed of the jealousy contortions:

> Apollo, pardon
> My great profaneness 'gainst thine oracle!
> I'll reconcile me to Polixenes,
> New woo my queen, recall the good Camillo,
> Whom I proclaim a man of truth, of mercy . . .
>   . . . how he glisters
> Thorough my rust! and how his piety
> Does my deeds make the blacker!   (III. ii. 154)

Paulina, announcing the supposed death of Hermione, is the voice of the Old Covenant:

> Do not repent these things, for they are heavier
> Than all thy woes can stir: therefore betake thee
> To nothing but despair. A thousand knees
> Ten thousand years together, naked, fasting,
> Upon a barren mountain, and still winter
> In storm perpetual, could not move the gods
> To look that way thou wert.   (III. ii. 209)

When the conscience counsels despair, it has become the
devil's voice; even the conscience, being human, may echo
the equivocations of 'the fiend That lies like truth' (*Macbeth*, v. v. 43). It is a momentary weakness, for Paulina
soon recovers and attempts to hearten Leontes, whom we
leave at the scene's end determined upon his penance:

> Once a day I'll visit
> The chapel where they lie, and tears shed there
> Shall be my recreation: so long as nature
> Will bear up with this exercise, so long
> I daily vow to use it. Come and lead me
> Unto these sorrows.   (III. ii. 239)

III – THE REDEMPTIVE POWER

BY THE transition of Antigonus' melodramatic vision we
pass to the kingdom of Bohemia to follow the fortunes of
Perdita. The comic scene in which she is discovered by the
two rustics has an undertone of mystical significance, which
in one sentence of the old Shepherd becomes clearly
audible: 'Now bless thyself: thou mettest with things
dying, I with things new-born' (III. iii. 116). This is fundamental. To bless oneself is to make the sign of the Cross,
and by the Cross those who are dying in sin are reborn to
righteousness. 'Regeneration' is the key to the play;[1] and
Perdita, the young child of Leontes, whom he cast out, is
in a sense Leontes born again – as Mamillius was the
Leontes who died. The finding of the child vies with the
Cleomenes and Dion scene for the honour of centrality;
the introduction of the oracle brings the first assurance of
divine overruling, but the finding of Perdita is the assurance of spiritual rebirth. Time the Chorus is not central
at all but a necessary mechanism of the plot, utilised for
further purposes already considered. The transference of
attention to Florizel and Perdita provides an opportunity

[1] So Dr. Tillyard: *Shakespeare's Last Plays*, p. 22.

of treating a number of subordinate themes closely related
to the main theme of regeneration. The sheep-shearing
feast must be studied with certain facts in mind: first the
key-word, 'regeneration', secondly the close interdependence of Leontes and his kingdom, and thirdly the symbolic
relation (based on the physical relation) of Leontes and
Perdita. Again, in the speech of Time the Chorus, Perdita
is spoken of as 'now grown in grace' (iv. i. 24), a phrase
at once reminiscent of Hermione. Florizel and Perdita
together also have a symbolic relation to Leontes and
Hermione; they are the positive affirmation of a state
which the elder pair, owing to Leontes' sin, can attain
only by the way of self-denial. United to this notion of
Florizel and Perdita as the positive, restorative power is
the old theme so frequent in Shakespeare and of major
importance in *As You Like It*: the opposition of court and
country, their interdependence and the priority of the
agrarian life in the scale of social values. Court life in
Sicilia was not very favourably presented; only a few opening words of the second scene in Act i gave some indication
of a gracious and polite social intercourse; and in Bohemia
Polixenes and Camillo are the skeletons at the sheep-
shearing feast. Country life on the other hand is not
uncritically lauded; there is nothing Arcadian about
Shakespeare's Bohemia as it is represented in the characters of contemporary significance. Autolycus by the
success of his trickery reveals the rustics' slow-witted
simplicity, to which the contents of a pedlar's pack are
more marvellous than anything the country has to show.
Small wonder that Autolycus speaks of his dupes as 'my
clown' (iv. iv. 616) and 'the rest of the herd' (iv. iv. 620)!
The Clown has few redeeming features; a taste for music
and a capacity for simple enjoyment. On the debit side
we may score his gullibility, his doubtful relations with
Mopsa and Dorcas, his abject cowardice when faced with
the courtier Autolycus and his *parvenu* attempts to play the
gentleman when later favoured by fortune. Sound rustic

values are mainly presented through the old Shepherd –
significantly a survival of an earlier generation, for he is
now 'a man of fourscore three' (IV. iv. 464). He displays a
shrewdly balanced judgment; though condemning in
general 'these boiled brains of nineteen and two-and-
twenty' (III. iii. 64), he can perceive that Florizel is more
reliable:

> They call him Doricles; and boasts himself
> To have a worthy feeding: but I have it
> Upon his own report and I believe it;
> He looks like sooth. He says he loves my daughter:
> I think so too . . .   (IV. iv. 168)

He has likewise a good opinion of Perdita:

> *Pol.:*   She dances featly.
> *Shep.:* So she does any thing; though I report it,
>   That should be silent:[1] if young Doricles
>   Do light upon her, she shall bring him that
>   Which he not dreams of.   (IV. iv. 176)

Nevertheless, Perdita is unfavourably compared with his
own 'old wife' whose picture, as the old Shepherd remembers her, presents the rural virtues more vividly than
anything in the actual feast then going forward:

> Fie, daughter! when my old wife lived, upon
> This day she was both pantler, butler, cook,
> Both dame and servant . . .   (IV. iv. 55)

Shakespeare clearly wishes it to be understood that in
thus presenting the rural virtues he is dealing with a
decaying tradition, for the old order, as we have said, was
already giving way before commercial exploitation and
its attendant evils. The old Shepherd alone preserves a
natural courtesy: the 'three carters, three shepherds,
three neat-herds, three swine-herds, that have made
themselves all men of hair' (IV. iv. 331) and 'call themselves
Saltiers' will, he fears, prove too much for the distinguished

---

[1] It is interesting to note an early version of the common excuse for praising
one's own: 'Though I says it myself as shouldn't'.

visitors: 'Away! we'll none on't: here has been too much homely foolery already. I know, sir, we weary you' (IV. iv. 340). There is dignity and almost tragedy, though not unmixed with humour, in his reaction to Polixenes' self-discovery and the unmasking of Florizel:

> O sir!
> You have undone a man of fourscore three,
> That thought to fill his grave in quiet, yea,
> To die upon the bed my father died,
> To lie close by his honest bones: but now
> Some hangman must put on my shroud and lay me
> Where no priest shovels in dust. O cursed wretch,
> That knew'st this was the prince, and wouldst adventure
> To mingle faith with him! Undone! undone!
> If I might die within this hour, I have lived
> To die when I desire.   (IV. iv. 463)

This lament betrays a whole rustic philosophy. There is the 'natural piety', respect for ancestors, which partly accounts for the countryman's hatred of removal and intense devotion to a small locality; there is respect for the Church's rites, especially as regards the disposal of the dead; and there is the feudal sense of order and subordination, which is outraged as much in the old Shepherd as in Polixenes by the disregard of social barriers displayed in the love of Florizel and Perdita. A mind of such calibre remains unspoiled by good fortune; it is the old Shepherd who administers the quiet rebuke: 'we must be gentle, now we are gentlemen' (V. ii. 164). These rustic virtues are clearly marked with Shakespeare's approval, for, although there are touches of humour in his treatment of the old Shepherd, there is an underlying gravity which comes out in the language of the old man himself and of others when speaking of him. Even in the burlesque court jargon of the three gentlemen there are a few phrases of serious import and one of them describes the Shepherd at the restoration of his foster-child to Leontes: he 'stands by', we are told, 'like a weather-bitten conduit of many kings'

reigns' (v. ii. 60). The pun ('reigns', rains) is significantly
agricultural, for, however kings and governments may
change, the old Shepherd, his rural toil and his rural
virtues, must stand by as the foundation upon which
civilised life is built.

Shakespeare, then, sees the rural life as fundamental;
but he also sees its shortcomings. Although we are to distinguish two generations of rustics and note that the elder
is preferred, in the more general contrast of court and
country we must take Shepherd and Clown together as a
balanced presentation of the advantages and disadvantages
of rural life. Indeed the weaknesses in the Clown and his
companions – dullness, vulgarity, triviality – are not solely
the result of changing circumstances; even the old Shepherd
is slow, rather uncouth, without the civilised graces when
contrasted with Florizel and Perdita. Country and court
are necessary to each other, Shakespeare seems to imply,
the sober virtues of the one and the graces of the other
compounding a perfect whole. It is the grafting process of
Polixenes:

> You see, sweet maid, we marry
> A gentler scion to the wildest stock,
> And make conceive a bark of baser kind
> By bud of nobler race.   (iv. iv. 92)

Florizel and Perdita represent this union; she in her festal
costume becomes a symbol of the country:

> These your unusual weeds to each part of you
> Do give a life: no shepherdess, but Flora
> Peering in April's front –   (iv. iv. 1)

while he,

> The gracious mark o' the land . . . obscured
> With a swain's wearing,   (iv. iv. 8)

symbolises the condescension of court to country, a seeking
by the court of the rural virtues. But Perdita herself, being
of royal birth and yet of country nurture, is the final
symbol of this union of court and country. To the old

Shepherd she is not quite up to the standard of his 'old wife', for royal birth, at least in Shakespearean biology, naturally unfits for menial tasks; yet she does take on her 'the hostess-ship o' the day' (IV. iv. 72) in obedience to her foster-father and, dressed in her 'May Queen' costume, is the ocular conjunction of royal and rural virtues. To Florizel she is no shepherdess but a queen (IV. iv. 5) and 'all her acts are queens' (IV. iv. 146). Polixenes has the same intuition of her nature:

> This is the prettiest low-born lass that ever
> Ran on the green-sward: nothing she does or seems
> But smacks of something greater than herself,
> Too noble for this place;   (IV. iv. 156)

and Camillo neatly defines the Perdita symbol by calling her 'the queen of curds and cream' (IV. iv. 161). So Perdita through her relation to Leontes takes back to Sicilia the qualities of the country; to Leontes a gentleman describes her as

> . . . the most peerless piece of earth, I think,
> That e'er the sun shone bright on,   (v. i. 94)

and this association with earth and sun is hardly accidental. As Leontes and his kingdom are one, we have here an acted parable of social regeneration, the reclaiming of an effete and over-sophisticated court by the incorporation of rural virtues which would guarantee a sound relationship between court and people. Polixenes also shared Leontes' failings; his tyrannous outburst against Florizel and Perdita witnesses to this and his attitude, coupled with the pseudo-aristocratical sneer of Autolycus – 'draw our throne into a sheep-cote!' (IV. iv. 808) – is sufficient to overthrow any suggestion that Bohemia is already satisfactorily Arcadian. It is by the marriage of Florizel and Perdita that both kingdoms are to be joined and in each a proper balance of court and country assured.

This theme of court and country – of social regeneration – is linked more closely than I have yet indicated to the

main theme of regeneration on the religious plane. A
number of minor themes constitute the link. As in
Mamillius Leontes died to sin, so Perdita is his new life,
and Florizel and Perdita recapitulate Leontes and Hermione but with a difference, for they represent the positive,
redeeming principle spontaneously active, whereas Leontes
and Hermione must tread a bitter road to their final
understanding. Florizel and Perdita, though symbolically
so close to Leontes and Hermione, present a strong contrast to them, a contrast parallel with and related to the
contrast of country and court. In the various aspects of
this contrast I find four minor themes. Florizel and
Perdita are a younger generation, unsophisticated, and
life-affirming; Leontes and Hermione are an older generation, sophisticated, and life-denying. My fourth theme is
less certain but I suspect the shadow of *Antony and Cleopatra*
and an implied contrast of Reason and Intuition,[1] though
Reason does not figure here as 'worldly wisdom', the vice
of Octavius Cæsar, but as the intellect functioning in
isolation from the other elements, faith, intuition, common
sense, which go to make up the normal mind. Leontes and
Hermione are, then, an older generation; their love was
sophisticated in the badinage of light conversation, in the
'knowing' jealousy of Leontes ('many thousand on's
Have the disease, and feel't not' (I. ii. 206)) and in the
dignified restraint of Hermione:

> I am not prone to weeping, as our sex
> Commonly are; the want of which vain dew
> Perchance shall dry your pities: but I have
> That honourable grief lodged here which burns
> Worse than tears drown.   (II. i. 108)

They are life-denying, Leontes in his jealous destruction
of his family and the penitential half-life that followed,
Hermione in a healthy and constructive way, submitting
in ascetic sanctity to the hermit's existence demanded by

[1] Cf. Tinkler; *loc. cit.*, p. 346; also *Shakespeare and the Popular Dramatic
Tradition*, pp. 122 *et seq.*

the oracle. Leontes shall be heirless until the finding of
Perdita; his penance for having wantonly destroyed his
family life is to live without wife and family until thoroughly
penetrated with the value of all he has wilfully forgone.
Florizel and Perdita are young (she is only sixteen), they
are unsophisticated, and they are life-affirming. In Perdita
the country theme takes on a deeper, religious significance
in a traditional association of spring, youth and sex. She is

> . . . no shepherdess, but Flora
> Peering in April's front. This your sheep-shearing
> Is as a meeting of the petty gods,
> And you the queen on't,   (IV. iv. 2)

says Florizel. Perdita is fearful that he may be discovered
in spite of his 'swain's wearing' (IV. iv. 9) but Florizel
reassures her, referring to the metamorphoses of Jupiter,
Neptune and Apollo in pursuit of love and, he adds,

> Their transformations
> Were never for a piece of beauty rarer,
> Nor in a way so chaste, since my desires
> Run not before mine honour, nor my lusts
> Burn hotter than my faith.   (IV. iv. 31)

The love of Florizel and Perdita is characterised by a
balance of strong sensuality and perfect chastity; there is
none of the Benedick-and-Beatrice, Rosalind-and-Orlando
type of thing – no coyness and coquetry, no 'thin ice', but
the frank avowal of love without sentimentality or evasion.
It is a love of body and soul, neither fleshly lust nor thinly
spiritual but involving the whole personality. Here is
Perdita's nearest approach to coquetry:

> O Doricles,
> Your praises are too large: but that your youth,
> And the true blood which peepeth fairly through't,
> Do plainly give you out an unstain'd shepherd,
> With wisdom I might fear, my Doricles,
> You woo'd me the false way.   (IV. iv. 146)

In reality it is frank praise of her lover, coupled with the recognition that all lovers are not equally to be trusted. Florizel's reply is quite serious:

> I think you have
> As little skill to fear as I have purpose
> To put you to't. (IV. iv. 151)

Perdita's flower speech is full of sexual significance:

> Now, my fair'st friend,
> I would I had some flowers o' the spring that might
> Become your time of day; and yours, and yours,
> That wear upon your virgin branches yet
> Your maidenheads growing. (IV. iv. 112)

The list which follows presents the flowers in sexual terms: daffodils that 'take The winds of March with beauty' (IV. iv. 119), violets associated with Juno and Venus ('Cytherea' in the text),

> . . . pale primroses,
> That die unmarried, ere they can behold
> Bright Phœbus in his strength – a malady
> Most incident to maids; bold oxlips . . . (IV. iv. 122)

Her list passes into a public declaration of love:

> O, these I lack,
> To make you garlands of, and my sweet friend,
> To strew him o'er and o'er! (IV. iv. 127)

'What, like a corse?' says Florizel, and Shakespeare gives her for reply a conceit in which passionate life is affirmed against the hint of death:

> No, like a bank for love to lie and play on;
> Not like a corse; or if, not to be buried,
> But quick and in mine arms.[1] (IV. iv. 130)

After this outburst there is an apology for her boldness,

---

[1] Critics have noted the parallel passage in Beaumont and Fletcher's *Philaster* (*Variorum Edition*, Vol. I, p. 211): [continued overleaf

G

but it is not long until Florizel, leading her to the dance, exclaims:

> . . . so turtles pair,
> That never mean to part,   (IV. iv. 154)

and she replies heartily: 'I'll swear for 'em' (IV. iv. 155). Frankness and faith characterise the love of Florizel and Perdita; mutual avowal, clear-eyed and unshakable. It is significant that from the first Perdita is aware of Florizel's identity – it is no romantic wooing with the prince *incognito* – and from the first Perdita is prepared for trouble from Polixenes. When it comes she can say:

> I was not much afeard; for once or twice
> I was about to speak and tell him plainly,
> The selfsame sun that shines upon his court
> Hides not his visage from our cottage but
> Looks on alike.   (IV. iv. 453)

She is not dazzled by rank; and she is prepared to bid her lover go, to waken from her dream in which she had never, like Leontes, lost hold upon reality:

> Being now awake, I'll queen it no inch farther,
> But milk my ewes and weep.   (IV. iv. 460)

Florizel is firm too:

> I am but sorry, not afeard; delay'd,
> But nothing alter'd: what I was, I am.   (IV. iv. 474)

If there should be 'violation of my faith', he says,

continued from p. 97]

> I could wish
> I rather were a corse strew'd o'er with you
> Than quick above you.   (IV. iv. 4)

Dr. Tillyard comments (*Shakespeare's Last Plays*, p. 10): 'The verbal echoes are too close to be fortuitous; and if, as is likely, Shakespeare was writing after Fletcher, he has transformed something thin and sweet into something so rich as to be scarcely comparable with its original'. We may indeed go further: Shakespeare has completely and challengingly reversed the original thought, and a melancholic desire for death has been transformed into a triumphant assertion of life. Playwrights sometimes indulged in pointed cross-reference at that period, and this reversal of the new escapist decadence may not have been entirely unintentional.

> . . . then
> Let nature crush the sides o' the earth together
> And mar the seeds within!   (IV. iv. 488)

These seeds are the Stoic and Neo-Platonic λόγοι σπερματικόι, the *rationes seminales* of the schoolmen; they are the forces of change, growth and fulfilment in Nature.[1] Shakespeare also uses the word 'germens' with the same meaning: Lear on the heath bids the elements 'all germens spill at once' (III. ii. 8); Macbeth bids the witches prophesy

> . . . though the treasure
> Of nature's germens tumble all together,
> Even till destruction sicken.   (IV. i. 58)

Lear and Macbeth in self-will would see the principles of life destroyed, but Florizel's faith is as immutable as the universal order itself. Unsophisticated in its clear avowal, life-affirming in its strong sensuality and perfect chastity, the love of these young people is a figure of regeneration. It is related to the country virtues and more deeply to the mystery of seasonal change, growth, blossom and fruition, in which the country virtues have their origin. Again, it is a spontaneous love; their firm faith is based on mutual intuition, not on the discursive reason. Florizel is advised by his 'fancy':

> . . . if my reason
> Will thereto be obedient, I have reason;
> If not, my senses, better pleased with madness,
> Do bid it welcome.   (IV. iv. 493)

Leontes' jealousy was unreasonable, but he fed it by specious rationality, even in his misery priding himself on a superior perception:

> Was this taken
> By any understanding pate but thine?
> For thy conceit is soaking, will draw in
> More than the common blocks: not noted, is't,
> But of the finer natures? by some severals
> Of head-piece extraordinary? lower messes
> Perchance are to this business purblind?   (I. ii. 222)

[1] V. Curry: *Shakespeare's Philosophical Patterns*, Ch. II, pp. 29 *et seq.*

Here in the jealousy rhythm's worst contortion is expressed the worst distortion of thought: 'finer natures' are those who apprehend such hidden adulteries. In Florizel and Perdita there is no such fine nature but a healthy wisdom which knows where it can trust, the reasonable intuition of a whole mind against the sharp but isolated rationalism of a split personality. Intuitive wisdom is redemptive. So, when Florizel gives up everything for Perdita, she accepts the sacrifice without a word, knowing it to be for the best. Her only comment comes later, when she says:

> I think affliction may subdue the cheek,
> But not take in the mind.   (IV. iv. 587)

IV – RESTORATION

IN Act V we return to Leontes who, having 'perform'd A saint-like sorrow' (v. i. 1), is now urged to remarry in order to provide his kingdom with an heir. But Paulina, the guardian of his conscience, keeps him to his vow. Now, in the fullness of time, Perdita returns, a 'peerless piece of earth' (v. i. 94), whose beauty vies with Hermione herself. Even the meaningless courtly hyperbole describes her in religious terms:

> This is a creature,
> Would she begin a sect, might quench the zeal
> Of all professors else, make proselytes
> Of who she but bid follow.   (v. i. 106)

Leontes greets Florizel and her with his mind full of past sorrow:

> Your mother was most true to wedlock, prince;
> For she did print your royal father off,
> Conceiving you –   (v. i. 124)

he is thinking of his own baseless suspicions of Hermione. Perdita he greets as 'princess, – goddess!' (v. i. 131), reviving the suggestion of 'Flora Peering in April's front' (IV. iv. 2).

This is hardly accidental, as he goes on to bid them wel-
come 'as is the spring to the earth' (v. i. 152). With strong
dramatic irony Leontes remembers the exposure of his
own daughter sixteen years before, in greeting this princess
who has crossed the sea to visit him:

> And hath he too
> Exposed this paragon to the fearful usage,
> At least ungentle, of the dreadful Neptune,
> To greet a man not worth her pains, much less
> The adventure of her person?   (v. i. 152)

This is a new Leontes, grown gracious and humble through
devotion. His next speech begins with the oracle motive,
for rhythm and language are directly reminiscent of the
short Cleomenes and Dion scene beginning Act III:

> The blessed gods
> Purge all infection from our air whilst you
> Do climate here!   (v. i. 168)

The religious note is continued in direct application to
his own case:

> You have a holy father,
> A graceful gentleman; against whose person,
> So sacred as it is, I have done sin:
> For which the heavens, taking angry note,
> Have left me issueless; and your father's blest,
> As he from heaven merits it, with you
> Worthy his goodness.   (v. i. 170)

The goodness of Polixenes is perhaps exaggerated here, but
the epithets ('holy', 'graceful', 'sacred', 'blest', 'worthy') are
an indication of the general theme and of the new character of Leontes. Even when a message reaches him of the
approach of Polixenes and he is properly informed of
Florizel's flight and Perdita's supposed low birth, his
demeanour remains gentle:

> I am sorry,
> Most sorry, you have broken from his liking
> Where you were tied in duty, and as sorry
> Your choice is not so rich in worth as beauty,
> That you might well enjoy her.   (v. i. 211)

He is so attracted by Perdita as to call forth Paulina's sharp rebuke, but it is her resemblance to Hermione which holds his attention:

                                                    I thought of her,
    Even in these looks I made.   (v. i. 227)

In the next scene we hear by report and through a veil of burlesque courtisms how Perdita's identity was made known and of the general reconciliation which followed. 'The oracle is fulfilled' (v. ii. 24); this is the keynote. It is a providential fulfilment, through what to human understanding is mere accident. Here and there a phrase of deep meaning stands out from its ridiculous setting: 'they looked as they had heard of a world ransomed, or one destroyed: a notable passion of wonder appeared in them' (v. ii. 16). This is a strong hint: providentially all has been or is to be restored; Perdita is returned, Mamillius is, as it were, renewed in Florizel, Hermione is soon to come to life, and the friendship of the two kings will be cemented into a union of the two kingdoms by the marriage of the heirs. Leontes and they all are born again – regenerate, 'ransomed' and restored; the old world of suspicion and hatred has been destroyed. The reference is clearly to the symbolism of Christian faith, in which Christ is said to have ransomed the world, though this world must be destroyed by fire so that the new Jerusalem may arise from its ashes, an eternal city.

The true climax, however, Shakespeare has reserved for his last scene, the final reconciliation, with Hermione as the central figure. It is not only the personages of the plot who are reconciled, but the contradictory themes, the life-affirming and the life-denying, are fused into a higher synthesis. Hermione and Perdita meet and we are to remember that it is the ascetic discipline of Hermione, her obedience to the apparently unreasonable message of the oracle, that has been the instrument, under divine providence, of her daughter's safe return. Florizel and Perdita, whose troth-plight was accomplished by the direction of heaven (v. iii. 150), have brought new life to Hermione and Leontes and to the whole no longer fatal kingdom of Sicilia; but this new life, this natural vigour, has been supernaturally bestowed and the gracious figure of Hermione, posed on her pedestal, reminds us that the natural is subordinate to and dependent upon spiritual power.

The restoration of Hermione, her coming back as from the dead, is a carefully prepared symbol of spiritual and actual resurrection, in which alone true reconciliation may be attained. Hermione's is not a genuine resurrection; since *Pericles* there has been no attempt to show anything even approaching a genuine resurrection on the stage. The very staginess of this 'statue' scene acknowledges the inadequacy of dramatic means. The poetry itself is quiet and serene in rhythm, simple yet profound in meaning. There is a certain generality and remoteness in the language; words of deep suggestion and religious potency link speech with speech in a common atmosphere of reverent awe. Leontes calls Paulina 'grave and good' (v. iii. 1) and speaks of 'the great comfort' she has been to him. She in replying speaks of his 'grace' (v. iii. 7). So it continues: 'life', 'sleep', 'death', 'soul', 'life of majesty', 'warm life', 'superstition', 'blessing', 'sorrow', 'joy', 'blood', 'life seems warm', 'affliction . . . comfort', 'breath', 'faith', 'marvel', 'Dear life', 'warm', 'magic', 'life', 'gods', 'sacred', 'graces', 'joys', 'exultation'. This brings us to Leontes' last speech and shows clearly how the atmosphere is built up and sustained. There is a holy quiet over the scene and Hermione revives to music, so often in Shakespeare a symbol of the heavenly and good, as all stridency suggested evil to him. But the strife of good and evil is not forgotten:

> O royal piece
> There's magic in thy majesty, which has
> My evils conjured to remembrance and
> From thy admiring daughter took the spirits,
> Standing like stone with thee.   (v. iii. 38)

There is an undercurrent here ('evils', 'conjured', 'spirits')
suggestive of the powers of darkness. It becomes overt in
Paulina:

> . . . but then you'll think –
> Which I protest against – I am assisted
> By wicked powers.   (v. iii. 89)

Later she commands:

>   Then all stand still;
> On: those that think it is unlawful business
> I am about, let them depart.   (v. iii. 95)

But reassurance follows quickly:

> . . . her actions shall be holy as
> You hear my spell is lawful.   (v. iii. 104)

This tinge of unease in the suggestion of black magic is
just enough to point back to the perennial moral and
metaphysical struggle in the world. In the resurrection the
struggle is past; the spell is lawful and actions shall be holy.
This last scene most obviously expresses the future life in
terms of the present; its rarified unearthliness is a foretaste
of heaven. The themes of redemption and regeneration,
now explicit, are related to a poetic suggestion of fulfilment
beyond this life. The scene operates retrospectively on all
that has gone before and so clarifies the expression, in
this old tale, of the Christian scheme from the fall of man
to his ultimate restoration in heavenly bliss:

> Bequeath to death your numbness, for from him
> Dear life redeems you.   (v. iii. 102)

CONCLUSION

CONCLUSION

SOME WRITERS on the history of civilisation or 'culture' –
Mr. Christopher Dawson, Dr. V. A. Demant, Mr. E. I.
Watkin – find that the main cultural problem is the relation between the natural and the supernatural, between
the horizontal plane of history, movement through time,
and the vertical line impinging on it and linking this
changing world with the eternal changelessness of God.
Mr. Watkin, in *Catholic Art and Culture*,[1] traces the relationship of natural and supernatural through many phases
from what he regards as the almost pure supernaturalism
of the pre-Nicene Church, when tension had hardly arisen,
to the present disruptive chaos out of which he expects to
emerge a finer and fuller synthesis than any hitherto
achieved. The conversion of Constantine, he notes, brought
the world into the Church and first raised the problem of
natural and supernatural in an acute form, and the monastic
movement began as a protest against increasing worldli-
ness. In the Dark Ages the Church had little opportunity
of seeing God in the natural order; her energies went
mainly into a struggle to preserve the essentials of religion;
but Mr. Watkin believes that in the Middle Ages a partial
synthesis was achieved, especially in the philosophy of
St. Thomas Aquinas and the poetry of Dante, though the
general tendency was still towards a puritan distrust of the
natural. The pendulum swung at the Renaissance with
its new respect for pagan antiquity, but this was ultimately
for the best, since it led to a more complete synthesis of
natural and supernatural than had yet been attained –
the age of the Baroque.

Mr. Watkin is dealing primarily with architecture, but
other arts are also considered and he extends the terms
'Gothic' and 'Baroque' to cover the general cultural

[1] Burns Oates, 1942.

characteristics of these periods. In the Baroque period he
finds a new interest in and respect for the natural, though
it is always perceived as a vehicle for the supernatural;
immanent and transcendent are held in balance. He admits,
however, that the synthesis is not quite achieved; there is
a persistence of the medieval tendency to dichotomise the
secular and the sacred, as in those poets who repudiate
their 'profane' verses when they turn to the cultivation of
sacred poetry; and sexual love, though freely used in
religious symbolism, is nevertheless condemned in itself by
religious poets, as leading only to misery and sin. Moreover,
in the treatment of the natural there is a constant habit of
wresting the natural material to make it more obviously
express a supernatural meaning, the imposition of alien
forms in wit and conceit; natural objects, instead of being
left to express the divine in their inherent beauty, are distorted by the intellect into religious allegory and emblem,
as the vegetable kingdom is transmuted into the animal by
the art of topiary. I have perhaps expressed this objection
more energetically than Mr. Watkin, who is clearly in
love with the Baroque, but he does at least say that 'it
had always contained . . . an element of artificiality and
external compulsion'[1] and he refers to 'the failure to realise
sufficiently the work of the Holy Spirit in nature'.[2] It seems
to me that the artificiality and even more the sensationalism and emotionalism of much Baroque art are due to
an attempt on the part of ecclesiastical interests to utilise
for religious purposes the new renaissance delight in natural
beauty and interest in individuality and the life of the
emotions. It was thus not a genuine mystical perception
operating through the natural but a forced diversion of
ordinary human feelings to supernatural objects. This is,
I believe, the usual point of view, with which I do not
think Mr. Watkin would wholly agree. In England the
cruder elements of the Baroque had relatively little

[1] *Op. cit.*, p. 134
[2] *Ibid.*, p. 137.

influence. Except for Crashaw the metaphysical poets have no important relation to Marino and the Marinists. Yet they too are frequently arbitrary in their treatment of the natural. When Benlowes observes that 'For May-games past, white-sheet *peccavi* is Winter's theme' – or indeed when the young Milton, years before, employing the same conceit, makes the earth 'hide her guilty front with innocent Snow', since

> It was no season then for her
> To wanton with the Sun, her lusty Paramour –

the association of seasonal change with the human cycle of sin and repentance, though interesting poetically, is hardly fair to the unfailing obedience and inevitable beauty of the natural order. Other poets of the time, however, contrast the order of nature with the disorder of human life; Vaughan grew envious of the birds, in whom a ray of divinity assured regularity in their matins,[1] and even the sober Herbert suffered momentarily from the quaint desire to be an orange tree.[2] But these were honourable exceptions.

Perhaps Mr. Watkin is unfair in seeing little but dissolution after the Baroque; rationalism in the eighteenth century and pantheist sentimentalism in the nineteenth, with the Church withdrawn into a defence of the *status quo*. I think there are hints in Victorian England of a fuller meeting of natural and supernatural, not only where we should expect it, in Christina Rossetti and Patmore, but at times in Tennyson despite his doubts and even more in Dickens despite the vagueness of his theology. But these are never fully conscious and it is to the late sixteenth and early seventeenth centuries that we must turn for anything like an adequate literary expression of Christian humanism – to Spenser, Jonson, Donne, Herbert, and most of all to Shakespeare.

[1] *V. The Morning-watch, Cock-crowing, The Bird*, all in *Silex Scintillans*.
[2] In the poem, *Employment*.

In Shakespeare we have a real synthesis of natural and supernatural without the usual Baroque distortions. He does not desert the secular for the sacred but finds the sacred deep down in the secular. And he does not impose an arbitrary symbolic pattern upon the natural; rather, taking the natural as it is and probing its deepest significance, he elevates it into a genuine and universal symbolism. This is most evident in *The Winter's Tale*, which may well be taken as the supreme literary expression of the Baroque – supreme just because it has none of those specially Baroque characteristics which place typical products of the period something below the rank of universal excellence: the Marinistic conceits and confectionary phrases, the sentiment and sensationalism of a Crashaw, or the tortured, arid ingenuity of Donne's rarer unhappy moments. Mr. Watkin defines the Baroque as Gothic in form but classical in material; it seems to me rather that the medieval and the classical co-exist in both form and matter. It is certainly so in *The Winter's Tale*. Technically, the Elizabethan drama combines the tradition of the medieval miracle plays with the methods of Plautus and Seneca as revived in renaissance Italy. There is a similar combination of ancient and medieval in the material of the plot and the attitudes expressed in the poetry. The situation is further complicated by the fact that the medieval inheritance must itself be subdivided into two contradictory strands, the ascetic tradition of the Church and the secular tradition of romance, going back to the Provençal Courts of Love with their organised opposition to the Church's ideal. I should say that Mr. Watkin, though critical, is rather optimistic in his estimate of the degree of synthesis achieved in the Middle Ages. Natural and supernatural were properly balanced in the Thomist philosophy but only on the most abstract plane. In concrete reality they were held by the medieval consciousness in tension rather than in synthesis, and St. Thomas himself is negative and restrictive on the subject of Christian marriage. Chaucer concludes the romance of *Troilus and Criseyde* with a *volte-face:*

> O yonge fresshe folkes, he or she,
> In whiche ay love up-groweth with your age,
> Repeireth hom fro worldly vanite!
> And of your herte up-casteth the visage
> To th'ilke God that after his image
> You made; and thinketh al n'is but a faire
> This world, that passeth sone as floures faire!
>
> And loveth Him, the whiche that right for love
> Upon a cros, our soules for to beye,
> First starf, and roos, and sit in hevene above;
> For He n'il falsen no wight, dar I seye,
> That wol his herte al hoolly on him leye!
> And sin He best to love is, and most meke,
> What nedeth feyned loves for to seke?

For nearly two thousand lines he has been entertaining the reader with a story of pagan love couched in the romantic terms of medieval chivalry, but now, not in the frigid formality of a stock conclusion but in poetry of real feeling, he calls him back 'home', as he significantly says, to the world-despising supernaturalism of the Church's popular teaching. This was home to the medieval mind; romance and the pleasures of the world were holiday indulgences, delightful and refreshing at the time but with a bitter after-taste. Even the worldly Chaucer never brings these divergent strands of experience into unity and, concluding the *Canterbury Tales*, prays forgiveness for his 'translaciouns and enditynges of worldly vanitees', under which head he names all his important poems, leaving unrepented only his translation of Boethius and his 'Legendes of Seintes, and omelies and moralitee, and devocioun'. As Mr. C. S. Lewis well says in this connection: 'We hear the bell clang; and the children, suddenly hushed and grave, and a little frightened, troop back to their master'.[1]

The story of Leontes has its classical origins overlaid with Hellenistic erotic romance and the chivalric romance

---

[1] *The Allegory of Love* (O.U.P., 1936, reprinted 1938), p. 43. Mr. Watkin also refers to Chaucer's repentance; *op. cit.*, p. 77.

of the Middle Ages, blended again with the pastoral tradition revived in renaissance Italy and introduced into England by Spenser, Sidney and Lyly. These strands are inextricably interwoven and it would be wrong to point to this or that incident as belonging more to one cultural phase than another. Medieval religion is represented in Leontes' penitence, his 'saint-like sorrow' (v. i. 2), and in the patient submission of Hermione, her quiet acceptance of unmerited punishment 'for her better grace' (II. i. 122) and the long years of her voluntary incarceration as almost an anchoress in the house of Paulina. There are even traces of what may be called the 'Gothick', in the eighteenth-century sense: Mamillius' tale 'of sprites and goblins' (II. i. 26) and a man who 'dwelt by a churchyard' (II. i. 30) might have been worked up by Mrs. Radcliffe (and much more effectively by Sheridan Le Fanu). Again, Paulina's picture of

> A thousand knees
> Ten thousand years together, naked, fasting,
> Upon a barren mountain, and still winter
> In storm perpetual,   (III. ii. 211)

is a good deal nearer Coleridge's imaginative vision than the orderly penance of medieval monasticism; the religious tradition itself is being romanticised. Antigonus' vision is as much Senecan as 'Gothick', another warning that we must not go too far in distinguishing the play's various elements; we are dealing not with a mixture but a compound.

There are, however, two principal components that we can distinguish by analysis: the Hellenic-medieval romance and the unromantic otherworldliness of orthodox medieval religion. These roughly correspond to the Florizel-Perdita and the Leontes-Hermione stories respectively. There is a certain sobriety in each of them, for the classical-romantic strain is fortified by its relation to the contemporary Warwickshire countryside and so built up into a worthy symbol of the natural over against the supernatural of the Her-

mione-Leontes ascetic theme and the overarching providence represented by the oracle. The great achievement
of Shakespeare is to have fused these two components,
to have succeeded where medieval poetry usually failed,
to have produced a synthesis where the Middle Ages perceived only a tension. For, as we have seen, it is the natural
virtue of Florizel and Perdita which restores the family
and kingdom of Leontes, yet that natural virtue is won by
the supernatural grace of Hermione's submission and
Leontes' penitence, and the whole compound process is
the work of Providence in individual and national history.
The natural order is itself good but, owing to human sin,
it must at times be repudiated in ascetic penitence, so that
it may return in greater fullness and purity. Here is the
original plenitude of the Christian way of life, in which
natural and supernatural dovetail into one another and
the humanist and the ascetic both find their place, since
'Wisdom is justified of all her children'.

This fusion of natural and supernatural is especially
apparent in Shakespeare's treatment of sexual love in
The Winter's Tale.[1] The medieval church, though avoiding
that complete condemnation of marriage which would
have implied Gnostic or Manichean heresy, seems to
have regarded the institution with some distrust. Mr. C. S.
Lewis points out in *The Allegory of Love*[2] the inadequacy of
the scholastics, even St. Thomas Aquinas, on this head –
they were concerned with sexual appetite and with
holy matrimony, not with love. Medieval sermons are
notoriously hard on women, daughters of Eve and tempters
of the unwary, while an occasional homily such as the
Hali Meidenhad[3] displays the obverse, railing on the
beastliness of man and the horrors of marriage and urging

[1] The brief history of love and marriage which follows has been slightly
altered from part of an article on Mr. Walter de la Mare's *Love*, contributed
by me to *The New English Weekly* for January 13th, 1944.

[2] Pp. 14 *et seq.* I am indebted to this excellent book for some particulars
and even more for its general discussion of the subject under consideration.

[3] Ed. Furnivall (Early English Text Society, 1922).

H

all young virgins to embrace the security of the cloister. Medieval marriages, at least in the upper classes, were usually contracted for solid business reasons, and this, together with the unsympathetic attitude of the Church, led to the cultivation of romantic love outside the marriage tie and its formulation as a convention of polite society in the Provençal 'Courts of Love'. Common sense must repudiate any suggestion that 'love' first appeared at a certain date in a certain region of southern France. In any civilised and monogamous society – in republican Rome, for example – there must have been a relationship between the sexes recognisable as love, especially in the lower orders, where problems of family and property did not arise. But 'romantic love' with its special code of behaviour almost parodying church order – with its casuistry and its prescribed devotion to living and highly secular saints – began in the courts of twelfth-century Provence. Thence its civilising influence spread over Europe, refining manners and reforming literature, while continuing to claim against the censure of the Church that 'marriage is not a justifiable plea for the refusal of love'[1] and even to add that true love is impossible between married persons.[2] There must have been a good deal that was bogus about the Courts of Love in actual operation, lust cloaked by an elaborate code of honourable behaviour, woman apparently exalted but really treated as the prize in an exciting and not too scrupulous game. The attitude persisted centuries later in the hollow professions of Petrarchan sonneteers under Elizabeth, so that it was a living reality at the time when Spenser, Shakespeare and Donne established a very different tradition.

Nevertheless, the chivalric code did have a humanising influence and in the later Middle Ages, though sexual license became more common (or perhaps more talked

---

[1] *The Code of Laws common to all the Courts of Love in the English, the French, and the Provencal dominions, of the Twelfth Century* is easily accessible in Walter de la Mare: *Love* (Faber and Faber, 1943), pp. 75-76.
[2] *V. The Allegory of Love*, pp. 35-36.

about), some of the professors of romantic love, like King
James of Scotland, or whoever it was who wrote *The
Kingis Quair*[1] sought marriage as its natural goal. Even
clerical writers unbent a little and a few poets among them
began to see love as a desirable ingredient in successful
marriage; *The Owl and the Nightingale* is pleasant on married
love[2] and satirists from Langland to the *Ship of Fools*
condemn loveless marriages contracted for worldly advantage.[3] It may be that the English Reformation contributed something towards the final fusion of romantic
love with the Church's doctrine of holy matrimony;
married parsons were perhaps more generally understanding in the matter. Thereafter the *Faerie Queene*,
Shakespeare's plays and Donne's gravest love poetry (no
one familiar with the period could take his cynical little

[1] There are several editions of this poem. It was edited by Skeat for the
Scottish Text Society in 1884, and this edition was revised in 1911. I chanced
to read it in the Glasgow edition, published in 1883 (printed, 1877).

[2] Ed. Atkins (C.U.P., 1922); *v.* ll. 1417-1602, pp. 120-135.

[3] William Langland: *Piers the Plowman*, ed. Skeat (Clarendon Press, 1886),
B text, Passus IX, ll. 151 *et seq.* (p. 278):

> And thus thourw cursed Caym ˙ cam care vppon erthe;
> And al for thei wrouȝt wedlokes ˙ aȝein goddis wille.
> For-thi haue thei maugre for here mariages ˙ that marye so her childeren;
> For some, as I se now ˙ soth for to telle,
> For coueitise of catel ˙ vnkyndeliche ben wedded . . .
> It is an oncomely couple ˙ bi Cryst, as me thinketh,
> To ȝyuen a ȝonge wenche ˙ to an olde feble,
> Or wedden any widwe ˙ for welth of hir goodis,
> That neuere shal barne bere ˙ but if it be in armes!

The Ship of Fools, translated by Alexander Barclay (Edinburgh: William
Paterson, 1874), Vol. I, p. 248:

> Suche ar they that for treasour and ryches
> Whyle they ar yonge in theyr chefe lustynes
> An agyd woman taketh to theyr wyfe . . .
> For they be maryd unto the vyle treasour
> And precious bagges, but nat for godly pleasour
> They haue no hope of children nor lynage
> Loue is there none . . .

It is noticeable that Langland does not in so many words condemn these
marriages as loveless, except in so far as that is implied in his 'vnkyndeliche'
('contrary to nature'). With Barclay, however, although he is himself a celibate
and a moralist, the word 'love' slips in quite casually.

jeux d'esprit seriously) established romantic love with its goal in marriage as an assured convention of English social life. Much of the credit must certainly go, indirectly, to Queen Elizabeth, in whose long reign women gained a higher degree of personal freedom and of education than ever before. An Elizabethan girl could be an intellectual companion to her lover; Beatrice, Rosalind and Viola are the last refinement of the type. Perdita is less sophisticated because more symbolic but she has plenty of good sense, and Florizel is not alone in perceiving it; even Camillo praises her:

> I cannot say 'tis pity
> She lacks instructions, for she seems a mistress
> To most that teach.   (IV. iv. 592)

Probably the Elizabethan or Jacobean young woman preferred this sort of praise to the conventional adulation she still received as the 'saint' of a despairing sonnet sequence. The Petrarchan phrases, wearing thin, were less affected by the best writers, except where wit could twist them into new meaning, and they survived mainly in minor verse until their ironical revival as the status of women declined after the Restoration.

✗ *The Winter's Tale* exemplifies the fusion of the romantic and the religious attitudes to sexual love. Shakespeare has happily discarded the excesses of the chivalric and Petrarchan tradition, the sighs and groans, the swooning and faded looks. Indeed, the healthy sensuality of Florizel and Perdita is a rare thing in romantic literature. Shakespeare has gone below the conventions of the tradition to its natural roots and again it is the union of natural and supernatural that he presents in the combination of sensuality and chastity displayed by the lovers. Perdita wants her lover 'quick and in her arms' (IV. iv. 132) but the remarkable frankness of her speech is equalled by the strong insistence on pre-marital chastity which stands out especially from this story of pagan times:

>   . . . my desires
> Run not before mine honour, nor my lusts
> Burn hotter than my faith,   (IV. iv. 33)

says Florizel as the lovers are first presented to the audience.
Here, as in other matters, Shakespeare comes out on the
side of the best social and religious hypothesis and helps
to confirm it as an English heritage. We have only to read
dramatists contemporary with him to see that lower views
of marriage were considered respectable, and Petrarchan
poetry continued under a Platonic veil to hint adultery
in high places. Shakespeare is the father – or at least the
most powerful advocate – of the pleasantly human love-
story with wedding bells as its happy ending, the sort of
thing that normal people still enjoy and approve when they
find it in literature or in life.

But we must remember Leontes and Hermione, whose
near-tragedy is also based on the sanctions of true love in
Christian marriage. Even Leontes' jealousy has something
to be said for it: if he had been right in his facts he would
not have been far wrong in his feelings of revulsion.
Hermione, of course, behaves as a true wife throughout
and their story reveals the tragic possibilities inseparable
from a high ethical and religious standard. These are
human beings in the full stature of humanity, not the
a-moral guinea-pigs of a modern psychological novel (or
perhaps we should now say a novel of the last generation).
It is the recognition of the deep value of sexual love which
leads in Leontes and Hermione to its renunciation during
so many years. The happy ending depends as much on
Hermione's self-denial as on Perdita's self-fulfilment, and
both are overruled by an oracular Providence which
directs their lives. The love theme thus reflects the more
general synthesis of humanism and asceticism we have
already considered. Natural and supernatural, humanism
and asceticism, the life-affirming and the life-denying, are
seen to be mutually necessary and interdependent in a
world where sin interferes with the pattern of natural

goodness and grace must redintegrate our fallen nature.
The medieval tension has become a synthesis and the
implications of the Thomist philosophy have been worked
out in the concrete detail of human life. In psychology,
the life of the senses and the life of the spirit; in devotion,
affirmation and denial of the flesh and the world; in society,
a balance of the natural agrarian life and the graces of
courtly civility which are nature too; in the broad sweep
of religious thought, the natural order and the supernatural, time and eternity; these are not alternatives but
mutually necessary and their integration brings a foretaste
of heaven into the life of earth. This is a statement in thin
abstraction of what seems to be Shakespeare's poetic
vision in *The Winter's Tale*. I think it is not too much to
claim that the play represents an important moment in
the history of Christian civilisation.

APPENDICES

APPENDIX A

Leontes' jealousy and his 'secret vices'

PROFESSOR DOVER WILSON is alone in denying the suddenness of Leontes' jealousy (except for a hint in Hudson's note quoted in the *Variorum Shakespeare*, p. 21). 'My own belief', says Dr. Wilson, 'is that the actor who plays him should display signs of jealousy from the very outset and make it clear, as he easily may, that the business of asking Polixenes to stay longer is merely the device of jealousy seeking proof' (*New Cambridge Shakespeare*, p. 131). By means of additional stage directions and in further notes on the scene he suggests that Leontes 'draws apart' during the dialogue in which Hermione urges Polixenes to stay and then comes forward just in time to hear and misinterpret her lines:

> The offences we have made you do we'll answer,
> If you first sinn'd with us and that with us
> You did continue fault and that you slipp'd not
> With any but with us.   (I. ii. 83)

It is true that Leontes draws apart; otherwise, as Furness says (*Variorum Shakespeare*, p. 13), there would be no need for his question: 'Is he won yet?' (I. ii. 86). But if Shakespeare had intended him to come up in time to hear and misunderstand a certain speech, he would surely have given some indication to that effect in the text. So important a matter is never left merely to stage 'business'. We should expect an aside – 'Is't so?' – and a phrase revealing the trend of his thoughts. And could he have misunderstood Hermione when she uses the plural so many times? A royal mistress would scarcely overwhelm an equally royal lover with such indications of her dignity. It is even less likely that Shakespeare should have intended Leontes

to be jealous from the outset; if he had, he would probably have brought him on alone at the beginning of the
scene to deliver an appropriate soliloquy. And if the urging
of Polixenes to stay had been intended as a trap, the
audience would certainly have been put on the alert by
means of soliloquy or aside. Later in the same scene, when
Leontes deliberately leaves Hermione attending Polixenes
into the garden, there is an aside which explains his
purpose:

> I am angling now,
> Though you perceive me not how I give line. (I. ii. 180)

It is unlikely that relatively naturalistic technique should
be used in the first lines of the scene and that conventional
treatment should have taken its place by line 180; indeed,
I know of no instance where Shakespeare leaves so important a matter to the inductive reasoning of the audience;
they had already enough to occupy them in following the
complexity of his verse.

Closely related to the jealousy problem is the question
of Leontes' 'secret vices'. Professor Dover Wilson believes
that Leontes had been a sexual libertine before the opening
of the play. In this he apparently follows Furness (v. the
note on 'Chamber-Councels' in the *Variorum Shakespeare*,
p. 43. Furness has no note on the 'posterns' passage discussed below.). The suggestion is important as it would
make the jealousy appear in rather a different light, not
a sudden falling into sin out of a happy, relatively innocent
state but the accumulated effect of previous sins. Also,
by implying that the marriage of Leontes and Hermione
was not wholly satisfactory even before Leontes' jealousy,
it would destroy the centrality of the latter and the
apparent pattern of the play, which runs from happiness
through sin to misery, then back through penitence to
happiness again. The following are the passages taken by
Dr. Wilson (in the *New Cambridge Shakespeare*, pp. 138 and
143) as referring to Leontes' secret vices:

> I have trusted thee, Camillo,
> With all the nearest things to my heart, as well
> My chamber-councils, wherein, priest-like, thou
> Hast cleansed my bosom, I from thee departed
> Thy penitent reform'd,   (I. ii. 235)

and Leontes' enquiry after the escape of Polixenes:

> How came the posterns
> So easily open?
> *First Lord:*   By his great authority;
> Which often hath no less prevail'd than so
> On your command.
> *Leon.:*   I know't too well.   (II. i. 52)

If Shakespeare had intended to suggest that Leontes had
'secret vices', he would surely have some special purpose
in doing so, for there is no hint of this in Greene's *Pandosto*
(where there is, however, later, the love of the father for
his unrecognised daughter, an unpleasantness which Shakespeare has gracefully turned into an innocent admira-
tion founded on her resemblance to Hermione). If, then,
the matter were so important to Shakespeare that he introduced it on his own initiative, he would surely have
expressed it much more clearly than he seems to do in
Dr. Wilson's rendering of these two passages. But in fact
there is no reason at all to interpret them in this way. In
the first Leontes merely says that he has made a confidant
of Camillo who has been, as it were, a confessor to him –
but, in spite of a popular and somewhat melodramatic
belief to the contrary, confessors do not limit themselves to
the hearing of sexual sins, and no doubt the King of Sicilia,
even if a perfectly chaste husband, would have a number
of private faults upon his conscience, or perhaps public
faults which he would not admit to in public council.
As for the second passage, posterns can be used for other
purposes than the admission of mistresses to the king; they
may admit spies or secret embassies, for instance. Leontes'
'I know't too well' need be no more than self-blame for

his supposedly misdirected trust, for we must remember
that it is Camillo again whose 'great authority' prevailed
to open them. Dr. Dover Wilson very remarkably presents
us with a Camillo who combines the role of grave and
priest-like rebuker of vice with the ill-assorted office of
pander-in-chief to his majesty! His interpretation of the
passages is unlikely in itself and would only serve to confuse
the clear outline of the play and obfuscate its meaning.

APPENDIX B

'The life to come'

'FOR THE LIFE to come, I sleep out the thought of it', says Autolycus (IV. iii. 30). Professor Dover Wilson has the following note on the passage (*New Cambridge Shakespeare*, p. 163): ' "*the life to come*" i.e. the future (not "the future life"). Cf. "the time to come" (IV. iv. 494)' [Globe edition, IV. iv. 508]. A more natural comparison is with the famous passage in *Macbeth*:

> . . . that but this blow
> Might be the be-all and the end-all here,
> But here, upon this bank and shoal of time,
> We'ld jump the life to come. (I. vii. 4)

Furness' note on the Autolycus passage (*Variorum Shakespeare*, p. 168), which Dr. Wilson seems in part to follow, explains it in the same way as he does but goes on to compare the speech of Macbeth quoted above and to maintain that it too refers only to 'his coming days' in this life; Macbeth, he says, hesitates to risk the peace of his 'days and nights' to come. This is somewhat misleading: the phrase 'days and nights' should be 'nights and days', it is not spoken by Macbeth but by Lady Macbeth and it occurs in an earlier scene (I. v. 70). In the *Variorum* edition of *Macbeth* (pp. 68-71) all the commentators quoted take 'the life to come' as the life after death, except Keightley and perhaps Tieck. Presumably Furness follows Keightley who comments: ' "The life to come" is not the future state, but the remaining years of his own life, as is manifest from what follows'. What follows are the lines:

> But in these cases
> We still have judgement here; that we but teach
> Bloody instructions, which, being taught, return

To plague the inventor: this even-handed justice
Commends the ingredients of our poison'd chalice
To our own lips.   (i. vii. 7)

I regret that it is necessary to consider the whole passage at some length in order to justify the usual interpretation. I suppose Keightley would paraphrase: 'If the whole affair should be completed with Duncan's murder, in this present brief moment of time (the night on which the murder is to be committed), I should not consider the future. But I am considering the future because these actions always have remoter consequences'. This is in effect to say that, if there were nothing to worry about in the future, Macbeth would not worry about it; it is too obvious to need saying. And does it not strain 'this bank and shoal of time' to understand it of a brief period? The difficulty is enhanced if we take the reading of the first folio, 'schoole', which is, I believe, preferable to Theobald's 'shoal'. 'Bank and shoal' is more 'poetic' in the stock sense but has less meaning; Shakespeare does not usually couple synonyms together. If we accept the original reading, 'bank' should not, I think, be taken as a school bench, which most commentators would have it to mean, but a judicial bench, probably from the Old French 'banc'. (I owe this valuable suggestion to the Reverend Gilbert Shaw.) The word was certainly current in this sense in Shakespeare's time (v. Oxford English Dictionary). Time is thus seen as the period of judgment, testing or 'crisis', and as a school; corresponding to these meanings we have later in the speech 'judgement here' and 'teach Bloody instructions'. With difficulty we could take Macbeth's moment of decisive action (the murder) as a 'bank and school of time', a moment of judgment and instruction, but how then are we to take the later generalisation:

But in these cases
We still have judgement here?

'Here' could hardly refer to the particular moment in each

of the hypothetical cases without intolerable strain. I believe that all the trouble has arisen from a failure to understand the colloquial illogicality of Macbeth's statement. Taking 'the life to come' as the life after death, a logical paraphrase would run: 'If there were no ill-consequences in this life, I should ignore the question of judgment after death' – absurdly implying that because there are ill-consequences in this life he does not ignore the life after death. But the colloquial turn of speech is a quite familiar compression: 'If there were no ill-consequences in this life [I should be quite satisfied, for] I should ignore the question of a future life'. I think there is little reason to doubt that the usual interpretation of Macbeth's speech is the right one.

Returning to Autolycus, we may now study the doubtful phrase in its context: 'With die and drab I purchased this caparison, and my revenue is the silly cheat. Gallows and knock are too powerful on the highway: beating and hanging are terrors to me: for the life to come, I sleep out the thought of it' (IV. iii. 27). Johnson's note on 'Gallows and knock' has been generally followed: 'The resistance which a highwayman encounters in the fact, and the punishment which he suffers on detection, withhold me from daring robbery, and determine me to the silly cheat and petty theft' (*Variorum Shakespeare*, p. 168). 'Beating and hanging' have been taken by other commentators as the equivalent of 'gallows and knock', which is very probable, and it thus seems plausible that Autolycus may 'sleep out the thought' of his future time on earth, since he had not put himself in the way of such terrors. The phrase 'on the highway', however, does not necessarily indicate highway robbery in the technical sense; the highwayman was more 'in the news' in Johnson's day than Shakespeare's. But as a vagabond Autolycus would spend his whole life upon the road and there is no reason to believe that in his reference to the highway he was dissociating himself from whatever mode of life the term implied. Again, even the

most petty theft was punished with whipping – Harman
reports that pilferers 'have been much lately whipped at
fairs' (*Caveat for Cursetors*, Cap. II) – and for theft of goods
above the value of twelve pence the punishment was
death. So, later, when Autolycus fears that he has been
overheard describing to the audience his success as a cut-
purse at the sheep-shearing feast, he exclaims aside: 'If
they have overheard me now, why, hanging' (IV. iv. 639).
It seems more than likely, therefore, that 'gallows and
knock', 'beating and hanging', are punishments he fears
because he knows himself to have earned them. In this
event his lively terrors would scarcely permit him to
'sleep out the thought' of the future in this world – and
indeed to interpret the phrase in this way would be to
make him contradict himself. But his fear of punishment
here may well have assisted him to ignore the possibility
of punishment hereafter. There seems, in fact, to be the
same contrast as in *Macbeth*: Autolycus fears the earthly
consequences of ill-doing but not the remoter consequences
after death. On this interpretation his speech would display
the antithetical pattern so characteristic of Elizabethan
and Jacobean prose: 'beating and hanging are terrors to
me: for the life to come, I sleep out the thought of it'.
It would appear that again the balance of probability is
in favour of taking 'the life to come' in its usual modern
meaning.

35/62